Young Rocky

Table of Contents

Introduction **4**
Chapter 1 *Castellani's Family* **6**
Chapter 2 *Young Rocky Castellani's
           Childhood* **13**
Chapter 3 *First Year of School* **17**
Chapter 4 *Junior High— Years
           of Confrontation* **41**
Chapter 5 *Love of Sports* **55**
Chapter 6 *Family, High School, Boxing* **59**
Chapter 7 *Falsifying the Birth Certificate* **75**
Chapter 8 *Basic Training* **83**
Chapter 9 *The Pacific Campaigns* **97**
Chapter 10 *Mission to China* **129**
Chapter 11 *Return to Pennsylvania* **145**
Chapter 12 *Turning Professional* **151**
Chapter 13 *Rocky's Management* **171**
Chapter 14 *Middleweight Aspirations* **191**
Chapter 15 *World Middleweight Aspirations* ...**196**
Epilogue **218**

D1585932

Introduction

This book tells the true story of Attilio *Rocky* Nick Castellani, Jr., from the time he was born in Luzerne, Pennsylvania, to the time he fought *Bo Bo* Olson for the Middleweight Championship of the World. The story is unique and colorful, as it is human.

It is unique in that it describes the life of a young man born into poverty of immigrant parents, the father working the harsh and cold mines of a bleak Pennsylvania town. It is colorful in that it follows the growth of this man as he goes through school and finally in the United States Marine Corps where, for the first time, he became aware of his personal strength, resiliency and intelligence: he fought in two of the most fierce battles of the Pacific— Guam and Iwo Jima, then off to China to represent the Marines in the military level boxing tournaments, winning championships and receiving congratulations from a Rear Admiral of the Navy. Above all, it is the human story of a young man who kept his head through the hardest of times, who, because of the basic goodness of his character, was able to overcome tremendous odds to become one of boxing most celebrated and cherished uncrowned heros.

Rocky was a pre-teenage fighter, a teenage great, and an under aged United States Marine. His career and exploits were covered in newspapers, magazine, radio and television, all the way from Guam, and

Shanghai, to his home town of Luzerne.

Rocky lived in the era of boxing greats such as Rocky Graziano, Jake LaMotta, Carl Bo Bo Olson, Sugar Ray Robinson, Jack Dempsey, Joe Louis, Rocky Marciano, and of other sports giants as Babe Ruth, Lou Gherig, Jim Thorpe and Jack Dempsey.

Here is a teenager who turned pro legitimately, who on earning his first dollar from *punching,* bought a box of doughnuts and an extra loaf of bread for his family. He was a streetwise kid with a sharp well-tuned body. He knew exactly what he wanted; fortunately, he had the physical equipment to go after it, though he did not succeed as he might have wanted to.

Starting on this magic carpet ride in the Wyoming Valley of Northeastern Pennsylvania, this skinny little Italian kid, who spoke broken English, fought his way into boxing's *Hall of Fame* as one of the youngest to attain that immortality.

China, here I come!

Chapter 1
The Castellani Family

Deep in the coal region of Northeastern Pennsylvania, in the belly of a mine shaft, dressed in the rough miner's clothes with a helmet on his head, Mr. Attilio Castellani Sr. paused for a rest. His face covered with sticky black dust, he brushed his forehead with one hand and began to think about what was happening in his home, wondering if his wife Rose, who had already lost two children, would carry their third child, hopefully a boy. His two girls, Maria and Anna, had survived and were rather healthy. He now hoped for a healthy boy to carry on the Castellani name. His daydreaming amidst the noise of machines, pick and shovels and human voices that bounced off the walls, soon came to an end when his stout foreman ordered him back to work.

"We're not in sunny Italy," he belted. "Here we work."

Mr. Castellani got to his feet, looked at the man, reached for the pick, and began digging. After a moment, he looked up at the foreman, who had been staring, with a grin on his face.

"Is there something wrong, *whap!*" the foreman asked.

Mr. Castellani shrugged his shoulders and continued to work. He did not understand much English, and certainly he had not understood that man's remark.

At home, Mrs. Rose Castellani, a thin, delicate woman with plenty of health problems, held her hand on her stomach, trying to keep herself warm. Dressed in plain clothes with a woolen dark shawl over her shoulders, she watched her two little girls play in the dimly lit kitchen, heated by a coal stove. At a given moment, when she felt the baby moving inside her, she followed the movement with her hand, and prayed to God that it be a boy, and above all, healthy. When Anna moved to the window to look outside, Mrs. Castellani told her to get down. When Anna insisted on looking out, Mrs. Castellani walked over and gently pulled on the sweater she had just knitted. With her hand still covering her belly, she looked outside at the bleak, snow covered surroundings, stepping to one side to avoid the cold draft sifting through the window panes.

"Madonna mia!" she exclaimed, *"dammi la forza...* give me the strength to carry this child," she pleaded, then turned to look at her two little girls absorbed in their play. "Thank God for them," she continued, knowing that to have them in the house gave her the will and the stamina to go on. She had already lost two children— both girls, and was thankful for what she had at this time, not realizing how very little she really had. Other than the sweaters she had knitted for the girls, and the colorful little ribbons she had put in each girl's hair, the rest of the clothes, as well as most of hers and those of her husband, were gotten through local charitable groups.

As she stared out the window, she daydreamed about life in the Southern Italian village where she was born and had grown up. But not all her memories were good. On one hand she liked the warmth of the climate, the friendship of the villagers, even the hard work on the dry and unfertile farm; on the other, she thought that no matter how much work those villagers did, their future was fixed— there was no future at all.

7

Covering her belly and rubbing over it gently, the tiny woman well realized her own sacrifice and that of her husband. No matter how dejected she might get, no matter how lonesome and cold, no matter how little food and clothes they would have at the moment, she was sure that sooner or later their lives would get better. Intuitively, she felt something special about the baby she was carrying. "He will be strong."

A Son!

May 28, 1927 was a special warm Spring morning, full of excitement in the little, tidy and unpretentious home of the Castellani. Two older women wearing colorful scarves from the old country on their heads, were busily boiling water on the stove. Rose, meanwhile, was in her bedroom waiting on the last labor pain.

"Come ti senti... How are you doing?" asked one of the women, a wide smile on her face.

"Il dolore... The pain is great. But what can you do? There is no joy without pain or sorrow... Ay! Ah, *Mamma mia! Madonna!"*

The women quickly rushed to her. On seeing Rose was ready, they each took their position. Amidst their screams, they began to pull the head until the baby was completely in their hands.

"E un bambino... It's a boy!" the older woman yelled with joy.

"Maschio... A boy! gleefully rejoinded the other.

As soon as they completed their chores and saw Rose was comfortably laying back nursing the child, who vigorously sucked at her breast, the women went to the kitchen.

"Hey, Anna... Maria, *venite dentro...* come back in. You have a brother!"

Full of hope, Mr. Castellani rushed home that evening, not knowing what to expect. His face still creased with black streaks of coal dust, he rushed into the kitchen, where his little girls were playing.

"*E un bambino...* It's a boy!" Anna screamed.

Apprehensively but with obvious curiosity, Mr. Castellani walked to the bedroom, pausing at the door. Rose looked up at her husband and smiled. He rushed to her side, his eyes fixed on their son, a healthy looking boy with long black hair.

"*Guarda che bello...* Look how beautiful he is," she commented proudly.

Mr. Castellani bent down and picked him up. Holding him in his arms, he began to talk in a low voice. "*Che bello...* how handsome, how strong. He's different from the other two. Look at his hair, Rose. Who does he look like?"

"He looks like you," she answered without hesitation.

"What are we going to call him?"

"Attilio!" she exclaimed.

"Attilio! My name?"

"Sure!" she exclaimed.

The next few years were very painful particularly for the Castellani and for the rest of the world as well. The stock market crashed and the great depression creeped into the very souls of the American people, especially the poor immigrants like the Castellani.

Young Rocky wasn't aware how poor his family was. His mother smothered him with love, kept him safe and sheltered, and did her best to give strength and courage to her family. She did everything possible to keep that baby happy, healthy and protected, with Attilio loving each and every moment. There was no *boogie man* in his world, no hate, no sorrow.

Unfortunately, he had no brothers to wrestle around with— (two brothers born after Attilio also died and were buried from the home in Pringle). So Rocky found himself growing up with three sisters and his poor but loving parents.

Rose prayed and thanked God for her healthy

9

children, doing her best in nurturing them all. She was especially happy over the boy. She saw him getting bigger and stronger— a solid good looking boy with dark eyes and black hair. He wasn't big by any stretch of the imagination, but possessed a certain presence about himself. He was a scrapper and both parents noticed this quality. Of course, Mr. Castellani was the prouder in that Attilio Jr. not only bore his first name, but also carried on the family name. Attilio Sr. liked to show off the boy on Sunday morning when he would dress with his only suit and tie and go to the town to chat with his friends. But as usual, the center of attention was always Attilio Jr.

Attilio Sr. especially liked to visit his brother, Michael Castellani Sr., who also lived in the neighborhood with his family. Michael Jr., who was sports oriented, would often muse over his cousin, young Rocky. But, throughout his life, Rocky called Michael Jr. uncle instead of cousin.

"What do you think, he'll be?" Attilio would ask.

"I don't know. Maybe sports."

"No!, not that," Attilio would answer with a smile.

In 1930, when Rocky turned three, America was in the middle of its great depression. Food was scarce everywhere and especially at the Castellani. Attilio continued to work at all kinds of jobs and was able to procure enough bread for his family. For many months, all they had to eat was bread. Luckily, for children born of a mother whose health had been and was precarious to say the least, they continued to grow without needing medical attention. Young Attilio was hardly ever sick, and the family seldom ever had cause for doctors. What's more, Rocky never complained about anything; he simply enjoyed playing either with his sisters or with the other little boys in the neighborhood, from sun up to sun down, seemingly never to tire. Rose, however, simply did not have the energy to follow the activities of her son. She wished she could have had the energy and the abundant strength her son was demonstrating.

Mr. Castellani also noticed the unusual energy of his son, but could not explain just what was behind it. Like his wife, he too would go into daydreaming about Perugia, Italy, where his family had come from, trying to remember his own childhood, but couldn't. The harsh reality of his present day America, (its streets paved with gold?), kept him from seeing anything clear, other than his need to go out and work at whatever to bring home the necessary food.

In dire poverty, nevertheless the Castellani did not feel the oppression of that great depression. They needed few material things to survive. What they had, which was more than many wealthy families had, was a sense of pride, of positive thinking and of encouragement. There was no despair, no pessimism. Though un-educated— as most Italian immigrants were— the Castellani felt a deep sense of spirituality, of belonging to a family unit which was growing and evolving more and more around that small ball of fire racing around the house.

"Where does it all come from," Rose would ask herself repeatedly, trying to stop him to calm him down, and to catch her breath. She would stand still and stare at young Rocky. In utter amazement, she wondered what she had on her hands, comparing her son's unbounded energy with the little bit she had, and concluded that, although she did not have much more time to live, she knew that her spirit would continue and mature in her little Attilio.

Chapter 2
Young Rocky's Childhood

In the Spring of 1932, Young Rocky turned five years old. It was also the time when he was introduced to the world of boxing.

Rose's energy was waning. Unable to contain her son, she asked her nephew, Michael Castellani Jr. (Mike Costello) to take the boy out for a while. She knew that Michael liked sports, and that Rocky would be happy to spend sometime with his cousin.

Michael quickly obliged by bringing the boy to the local gym. In seeing two young boxers sparring in the ring, the boy became fascinated. Impressed, he kept on staring at them while his cousin went on with his routine of weight lifting and other exercises. When Michael asked him to stay with him, young Rocky chose to look at the fighters, mesmerized by their agility and by their courage to face each other in battle. Looking at each fighter throwing fists, he unconsciously found himself lunging with his hands.

Rocky's cousins, Mike, Eddy and Mickey, also worked out in the Swoyerville Owen Street school basement, with Mike Surban doing the training and managing the activities.

Across from the ring, Michael, who had done a little boxing himself, couldn't believe how wrapped up his little cousin was with the boxers. "Hey, Attilio, do you want to fight?" Michael asked in laughter.

Rocky turned around without an answer. He silently looked at his uncle, then immediately turned toward the boxers and continued to stare seriously.

When the two boxers left the ring, Michael approached Rocky and asked him if he wanted to get in the ring with him. Jubilantly, the little boy accepted. Michael picked him up by the waist and hoisted him between the ropes. Inside, Michael began to clown, throwing his fists in the direction of the boy, who instinctively ducked and swayed to avoid his uncle's harmless blows.

After about twenty minutes, Michael called it quits. "Let's go home," he said.

"No, uncle, please..."

"I'll bring you back here some other time, OK?"

Disappointed, Rocky agreed. On the way home, the boy felt a certain exhilaration— an excitement he had never felt before. He knew he was going to be a boxer.

That night, he saw it all in his dream, and the dreaming was boxing.

Bright and early the next morning, Young Rocky was already running to the park to play with his friends. But this day, things were different. Instead of playing with his buddies, he sought out the older boys and men to ask them about boxing.

At the supper table, that evening, Rocky began to ask the same questions of his mother and father, half in English, half in Italian— a very normal thing for a child exposed to two languages. Rose, of course, was flustered and could not even comprehend what her boy was saying. Mr. Castellani, however, placed his hand over his son's shoulder to calm him down amidst the giggles of the girls who found the whole thing very amusing.

"*Stai fermo...* Keep still, son. Take it easy. What's this boxing you're talking about? Did your cousin do something to you?"

"No, pop, no! I like him. I like to go with him to

the gym. It's fun. I like boxing."

"Boxing? Broken nose! Scars on face! Blood! No, no son, no boxing for you. You have the face of an angel. I'll speak to Michael and tell him to try other sports. There's baseball— Baby Ruth..."

"No dad... boxing!" he said with unusual resolution, as though the answer was coming from another person within the boy, for he was too young to speak with any kind of conviction.

On getting that answer, Mr. Castellani shrugged his shoulder. "What is meant to be will be."

"*Oh, Maria Santa...* Holy Mary!" exclaimed Rose. "You, no boxing."

Through the forthcoming years, Rocky kept on visiting the gym with or without his uncle, and always working on or with the various boxing equipment— fighting, boxing, jumping rope, sparring and just getting involved with all kinds of boxing actions. One day, while at the gym, Rocky approached his uncle.

"Uncle Michael, you know what I want for Christmas?"

"You bet I do."

"What?"

"*Una palla...* A baseball!"

"Come on, you know."

"I know. You want a pair of gloves. I'll get them for you. But don't tell your mother or father."

On hearing those words, Attilio jumped to his cousin and wrapped his arms around his neck, thanking him in advance for the future gift. Meanwhile, the boy continued to train by himself. Driven by an inner force, young Rocky found himself shadow boxing in his room. Before going to bed, he always said his prayer, always following that ritual with a few minutes of shadow boxing. Often, however, his mother would hear the noise and tell him to go to sleep.

15

Chapter 3

First Years of School

Although his older sisters were in school, and Mr. and Mrs. Castellani had already had enough experience with the various teachers and student friends, Rocky was to find the Pringle Elementary School setting perfectly suited especially for his athletic needs. Although he had had many scraps with the other boys in the neighborhood park from time to time, now in school, with the higher concentration of boys, Rocky would find himself in more frequent and challenging situations.

With Primo Carnera the Heavyweight Champion of the world, and with the intense interest in boxing by Rocky, the conversation was always on boxing. At school, he became somewhat of a braggart— though in a quiet way, and almost always ended up wrestling with the boys who would criticize Primo Carnera. One particular first grader, who was a few inches taller and heavier by several pounds— during a short outside recess— got the better of Rocky in a wrestling match that saw the boy get a good head lock on Rocky, amidst the cheers of several other first and second grade boys who were obviously opting for the other boy. Realizing wrestling would not do, Rocky finally broke the hold and quickly jumped to his feet, his fist

17

tight and aiming at the face of his opponent.

"Come on!" Rocky challenged, amidst the cheers of the boys who had gotten the attention of the teacher.

The boy burst forth with his fists up, but only to receive a precise blow to the chin that floored him. On seeing him on the ground, Rocky stood back apprehensively. Suddenly, everyone was silent, except for Mrs. Brown's menacing words.

"You both report to the Principal this very moment. I will see to it that you are punished."

The two boys, with heads bowed, walked to the office, while the other boys remained in place startled by Rocky's punch.

Inside the office, the Principal first listened to Mrs. Brown and then the boys. Afterwards, he decided to deny recess privileges for one week. "But," he said sternly, "the next time, I'll have your parents in this office should this fighting continue. Do you understand?"

"Yes sir!" answered the boys in unison.

The following couple of years were somewhat uneventful for young Attilio, except for many friendly scraps he continued to have outside school. During these encounters, he always found himself using his fists and almost always winning, to the point that the other boys knew they couldn't match him, and no longer challenged him. In the meantime, Rocky began to make friends with several of his peers and actually enjoyed going to school.

His mother, however, got more and more sick. In spite of her bad health, she had a fourth child— Yolanda (Lonnie), but still managed to keep the four kids neat and clean. Mr. Castellani, on the other hand, kept working in the mines, finding life somewhat less oppressive, in that he was making slightly better wages and was therefore able to better provide for his family, even though they were still wearing clothes received either from charitable organizations or the WPA.

"Da dove prende tutta questa energia... Where does

he get all this energy?" he asked his failing wife, late one cold winter evening.

"*Da Dio...* From God. He has been good to us. Look how well the children are growing after all we've been through. God will help them."

"And you, I see you getting more and more sick. What is the matter, Rose? Is there anything I can do? How about a doctor?"

"It's this terrible cold weather that's wearing me down. I'll get better in the spring."

With Yolanda at home, Attilio in the third, Anna in the sixth and Maria in the seventh, the four kids began to walk to school to begin the year. Well groomed, they left the house under the watchful but sad looking eyes of their mother.

On the way, Maria grabbed Attilio's hand. Anna, however, protested in that she wanted to hold her brother's hand, and getting her way. To avoid discussions, Maria said nothing.

Pringle Elementary School was no different that year than in the past. The principal was the same; so was Mrs. Brown, except that she had gotten a little heavier, her hair more gray, and her complexion lighter.

One day, while doing a unit on history, Mrs. Brown asked the kids to give names of famous individuals who had made important contributions to America. Immediately, the kids responded by raising their hands. Mrs. Brown called on the kids, who all gave the names of their famous heroes— Lincoln, Washington, Jefferson, Lafayette, Franklin, Columbus, etc. Satisfied with the response, Mrs. Brown then asked to identify the national origin of those famous people. Quickly, the kids raised their hands, except for Rocky and his bench buddy Antonio, who, aside from the fact that he too was the son of Italian immigrants, had cross eyes. In any event, Antonio was somewhat ahead of the other kids on history because his father, who

19

had gone to the fifth grade in the old country, had continued to teach the Italian language and culture to his children. In class, however, he was always quiet, never volunteering any answers unless forced.

"Alright, kids, we have seen that many of our heroes come from France, Holland, England, Germany, Spain, and even Russia. No one has mentioned Italy." On seeing the students looking at each other puzzled, and noticing that no one was coming forth with a name, she told the class that they would go on with that kind of game from time to time in the future. "Now, however," she said, on seeing everyone attentive, "we have to get back to our books. Today, we want to learn more about the Pilgrims. We want to know more about the Mayflower— the ship the Pilgrims used to sail to America. Please turn to page twenty five and let's start looking at the picture of the ship..."

"How about Columbus?" blurted out Antonio nervously, his eyes pointing closer together.

Almost simultaneously, the kids turned their heads to the back of the classroom, amused by Antonio's unexpected intrusion. A few began to giggle. Startled but composed, Mrs. Brown quieted the kids by asking them to face front.

"What about Columbus?" she asked with a slight smile.

Before Antonio had a chance to speak, a girl in the front row volunteered the answer: "Columbus sailed from Spain."

"He was Spanish," interrupted another.

"Well, Antonio," asked Mrs. Brown.

"He was Italian," Antonio answered, amidst the giggling, hissing and the somewhat ridiculing classmates.

"Alright class," interrupted Mrs. Brown. Let's open our history book for a moment. The very first chapter, The Exploration of North America... Got it everyone? Janet, please read the first paragraph."

After Janet finished the paragraph which stated that Columbus had sailed from Spain after the Queen had sold her jewels to buy the ships, Mrs. Brown asked Antonio for comments. With Rocky looking embarrassed at Antonio, Antonio said, "It don't say he was from Italy."

"Well?" Mrs. Brown commented, holding her hand out to keep the kids from being noisy.

"He was Italian," Antonio answered, then put his arms on the desk and sunk his head down into them, while Rocky looked in disbelief.

"How about you, Attilio, what do you know about Columbus?" she asked, with an obvious attempt to diffuse what turned out to be an awkward situation.

With his eyes widening, Rocky raised his shoulders up practically around his head and said, "I don't know."

"Alright class, we'll let it go at that. Let's get back to our Pilgrims and their Mayflower."

Third grade was a good year for Rocky. Outside the few minor incidents within and outside school, he had had a good time especially with the boys. Although he enjoyed playing all kinds of sports, outside of boxing he preferred baseball, just about any position but catcher.

In the winter of that year, after a blizzard that left over a foot of snow, young Rocky and his three sisters went to school as usual, with Anna holding his hand, and Maria that of Yolanda. At the corner, just before turning toward the school, one of his buddies with whom he had thrown snow balls a few days before suddenly appeared from one side with a couple of snow balls in his hands.

"Hey, come on Attilio, how about a snow ball fight?"

"No!" Anna answered, holding on tight to her brother's hand.

Before Rocky could answer, the boy hurled the

snow ball which landed squarely on young Rocky's head, causing a great big grin of satisfaction on his buddy.

"Let go, Anna, let go!"

After a short struggle, Rocky got away from Anna's clutches. He quickly went for the snow and began what turned out to be a barrage. Unfortunately, one of the snowballs fell on Yolanda's face causing her to cry. Seeing what had happened, young Rocky stopped and called a truce.

Maria quickly turned to Yolanda and began to wipe off the snow, while her little brother looked on.

"See what you did!" Anna snarled. I'm going to tell *Papa* when he comes home."

After getting their composure, the four began to walk toward school. Anna, as usual, grabbed Attilio's hand. This time, however, young Rocky resisted.

"No more holding hands," he said. "I'm no little kid."

Surprised, Anna and Maria looked at each other, then looked down at Yolanda, who stood silently— a tiny tear still on her face.

At school that day, things did not go too well. The other kids had heard of the snow fight and challenged Rocky to another after school. Expectedly, Rocky, Antonio, and several other kids of Italian background formed one group, while another bunch of mixed ethnicity formed the other. On getting outdoors, but still on school ground, the two sides began to throw a barrage of snow balls, for the most part landing on the heads of little girls, making them scream to the delight of the boys. The principal, who had been standing by his window, saw the incident and rushed outside to stop it. On seeing him, they immediately took off, except for Rocky, who had been looking another way.

"You're coming to the office with me," the Principal ordered.

Rocky, with his three sisters behind, made his way to the office where he learned that his father would be called in the next day, the principal making sure that Rocky understood the hardship he was imposing on Mr. Castellani because of that incident.

Outside, Mrs. Brown, who had also seen everything, decided to check things out. On learning the punishment the principal had meeted out, she asked him to let her punish the offender.

"You're a lucky boy, Attilio," he said.

With tears in his eyes, he followed Mrs Brown to her room, with his three sisters closely behind.

"Attilio, no more shenanigans, do you hear?"

"*Shenanigans?*" he repeated, not knowing the word.

"Yeah, I know, you little Italian boy," she said with a smile, wanting to say 'precious' instead of 'little'. "You go home, and no more snow balls. Is that clear?"

"Thank you," Rocky answered, a smile on his face.

Immediately out into the corridor, Anna once again attempted to grab his hand, to no avail.

That evening turned out to be colder than usual. At home, Mrs. Castellani tried everything possible to keep the stove going, but somehow, she simply could not warm herself up. On seeing her children suffering from the cold, she immediately had them put on extra sweaters and began to cook an early supper.

"*Un buon piatto di pasta...* A good dish of pasta will warm you up," she said. "Maria, come help me. We'll make extra. *Papa,* I'm sure, will also be hungry."

As usual, Mr. Castellani arrived home on time. This evening, however, a little more hungry than before. The cold weather was just a bit too much.

At the supper table, Mrs. Castellani, who was still cold, asked her husband to go fetch more coal.

"I want to make sure we'll have enough heat for the night," she said.

Mr. Castellani quickly obliged. On his return, however, he noticed something was wrong, but couldn't understand what.

"*Stai bene...* Are you well, Rosa?" he asked, his eyes looking deeply into hers.

The woman turned away slightly so as not to be seen. In her heart she knew she was not going to last long, and did not want to reveal her feelings. She thought when her brother asked Attilio Sr. to join him in the trip to the port of New York on her arrival to America from Italy.

"Sto bene... I am fine," she answered. "Do you know what I would like to do this evening?"

"What?" Mr. Castellani asked.

"Let's talk about our villages, the old country. I want the kids to know where we come from. I want them to know a little about their grandparents, aunts, uncles and cousins. Someday, who knows, Attilio may want to visit Italy, and he, together with his sisters should know where we came from and who our people are."

With that, the six sat around the table, eating on various other pastry that Mrs. Castellani had baked, and began to talk about the old country. Mr. Castellani explained that his people came not far from the city of Perugia— the city founded by the Etruscans long before there was a Rome, that the city had two very famous universities, but that neither she nor his brothers nor sisters ever went to school beyond the first few years of elementary. He remembered how they spent Christmas, going to visit the *Presepe...* the manger scenes in different churches, and how on the 6th of January they exchanged gifts and what they put in the stockings. Young Rocky Castellani was intrigued by the custom of putting rocks or coals in the stocking of kids who had misbehaved during the year.

Mrs. Castellani also told her story, how she and her family came from southern Italy— perhaps the poorest section of the peninsula, where life was very hard, where, no matter how much one worked, there simply was never enough to better one self.

"How about America?" Maria asked.

"America is different. I have been wanting to tell you this. We want to get a new house. When, we do not know. But we plan to buy a house. Isn't that right, Rosa?" he asked proudly.

"*Si, si!*" Rose answered, her head bowed. "We want you all to have your own home, something we couldn't have had in the old country, at least not on our own and not as fast as we can do it here."

So, in the Spring of 1937, Mr. Castellani first rented and then purchased his first home— 816 North Street in Luzerne— a duplex so he could rent half to help with the payments. When the paperwork was completed, everyone pitched in for the move, especially the kids, including Michael Castellani (Costello) Jr. In less than two days, between Saturday and Sunday, the Castellani family was moved in. Sunday evening, they all relaxed in the larger home while Rose and Maria prepared a special supper— ample dishes of pasta, followed by a few *cotolette...* broiled potatoes and salad. Mr. Castellani had gotten a bottle of home-made wine from a friend, and with his brother and the others, enjoyed it all.

"Attilio," Mr. Castellani said, "do you want to try some wine?"

"Sure," young Rocky answered, proud his father had asked. But on tasting it, he made a face, to the delight of the girls who giggled at their brother's funny expressions.

Mr. Castellani, on moving to the new house, also moved into a new neighborhood. Not that he had cared much who lived next door— he was too busy working morning to night, so didn't really have the time to get to know his neighbors. And only later, he learned that he had moved into a section where his family was in the minority— the majority consisting of recent immigrants from Poland and Lithuania.

Now ten years old and in a new neighborhood, young Rocky quickly made friends with other boys. In no time, he and his buddies claimed a spot of land for themselves on an abandoned concrete slab where an old garage had once stood. After hammering one pole for each of the four corners, they tied clothesline rope around each thus making their own boxing ring. There, Rocky and his friends began to spar in earnest, using equipment they either got or made themselves. A motley crew in the eyes of any adult, the boys however were proud of what they did and were even more proud about their boxing. Those young kids were not aware of the fact that instead of just learning the craft of boxing (and not brawling on the streets), they were acquiring their crafts in a somewhat self imposed controlled situation. What's more, Rocky, the main instigator, wasn't even aware he was showing leadership capabilities; for, it was he who got the idea and had seen it completed. More amazing was the fact that this little skinny Italian kid was so much at home with his new Polish, Slovak and Lithuanian friends. Things, however, did not go Rocky's way all the time.

There were always reasons to have arguments which resulted in fist fights and wrestling matches. And of course Rocky, being in the minority, often got the worse of it. What he couldn't stand, however, was the involvement of the older boys who picked on him, especially going and returning from school, resenting being called the usual denigratory ethnic names. At first, Rocky did not understand what they meant. But soon he had an idea and decided to retaliate.

One evening, on seeing two men who had just left the local *Beer Garden* (as the bar rooms were called in those days), and noticing they were staggering, he decided to make his move. The two men were the fathers of the two boys who always picked on him on the way to school.

After locating a dimly lit spot on the street, Rocky hid behind the wall of a house high on the stairs overlooking the sidewalk, but well within reach of anyone passing by. With the stick of a broom handle firmly in his hands, he waited for the same men to walk by— usually always at about the same time, for they stopped at the Beer Garden immediately after work and would go home after having had their drinks— something Mr. Castellani was not in the habit of doing. On seeing the two big men wobble forward, he raised the broom. Just as they came within reach, he beat on their heads and immediately ran off through the back way. The confused men were so startled that they failed to see who it was let alone where the broom blows had come from.

When the same thing happened to a few other men on different occasions, word got out as to the culprit.

One evening, while Mrs. Castellani was preparing supper with her three daughters and Rocky was supposedly doing homework in the bedroom, they heard a lot of commotion on the sidewalk. Mrs. Castellani walked to the balcony to see what was going on and was met by a group of men, women and children complaining about young Rocky hitting the men on the head and running. Mrs. Castellani, who spoke little English, understood only too well what was happening. With her husband not at home, she decided to take things into her own hands. Rushing inside, she ordered the children to their rooms. Then, running over to a closet, she reached up to the upper shelf for the shot gun Mr. Castellani was saving for his hunting. Being sure the weapon was empty, she rushed to the balcony.

"*Andatevene...* Go away, or I'll shoot all of you," she yelled.

Not expecting that kind of confrontation, the women first, then the men, decided it was better to leave, to seek other ways to solve the problem.

Curious as he was, but knowing the commotion had somehow to do with him, Rocky sneaked to one side. On seeing his mother with the shot gun in hand facing the group of people, he felt awed. He couldn't believe his eyes. There was his mother— practically smaller than the gun. As sickly as she was, with fire in her eyes, there she was protecting him and his sisters.

27

When the people had disappeared, Mrs. Castellani returned to the kitchen, looked at her speechless children, and went directly back to the closet to put away the weapon.

"*Non dite nulla...* Don't say anything about this to your father, understand?" she told her children, who were still under shock. "*Niente!...* Nothing, understand!" she repeated as they nodded their heads with approval.

November 1937 turned out to be unusually cold and cruel. After supper, one evening, with the children in bed, Mrs. Castellani told her husband how sick she was, that she could no longer go on.

"What's the matter?" he asked as he looked at his diminutive 38 year old wife weighing less than 100 pounds. "What can I do?"

"Attilio, I don't think there's anything anyone can do. You know I have tuberculosis and I can't stay here any longer."

"*Dio mio!...* My God! What will that mean for us?"

"Only that I'm not going to be around much longer. You have to get used to go on without me. I taught Maria and Anna as much as I could. They can cook and clean the house. You will have to take care of the rest. I'm sure you will get along. Do the best you can; keep on loving them. I know you can also be as good a mother as you are the father."

"Stop talking this way."

"No, it's all set. I've made arrangements to be admitted to the Sanitarium. I didn't say anything to the children except to Maria. I told her that I'm very sick and that I will soon have to go away, possibly never to return."

At those words, Mr. Castellani got a lump in his throat. In a few moments, tears began to slide down his face as he sat silently looking into the hollow eyes of his wife. "My God, no!"

"*Attilio, sai...* You know the last thing I want is to

leave you and the children. But God has willed it so. There isn't anything I can do."

"*Lo so...* I know! I know that you would never leave your children. No one does, not even animals."

"Attilio, you will take care of them."

"*Si, Rosa...* I will. I will take care of them," he assured, tears rolling down his face, causing Rosa to cry. He embraced her tenderly. "Is it all set for tomorrow then?"

"*Si,*" she whispered.

"*E i bambini...* And the children, when will you tell them?"

"*Domani mattina...* Tomorrow morning, before they go to school."

The next morning, Rosa got up earlier than usual to prepare breakfast. When she was ready, she got the kids up and dressed them. After they finished breakfast, she asked them to remain seated for a few moments. Knowing what she was going to say, Mr. Castellani began to cry, but turned around so as not to be seen.

"*Voi sapete...* You know that I am very sick. Today, I will be going to the hospital. Chances are very good that I will not come back."

"Mommy!" exclaimed Anna. "What are you talking about?" she asked with obvious desperation, tears on her face.

"Mother!" little Attilio blurted, "you cannot go."

"*No, figlio mio...* No, my son, I have to go. If I stay here, I will not be able to take care of you, and you know how much I love you all. You have to be strong. You all have to promise me that you will get along, will help each other and be good. Will you promise that?"

"*Si, Mamma...* Yes, Mamma, I will," young Rocky answered, followed by Maria, Anna and then Yolanda.

"*Va bene...* Fine, then," Mrs. Castellani said, her heart pumping, but still able to hold back her tears.

29

"Maria, get your lunches, dress and go to school. When you come back, don't ask where I am. Just go right on with what you have to do. *Forza, andate...* "*Go on, go!*"

Silently, and with tears in their eyes, the four got up. After getting their things, they stood by the door. Mrs. Castellani hugged each one and send them out one by one. When they were on the sidewalk, she closed the door and stepped to the window to look at them, tears streaming profusely down her face. Attilio Sr. put his arms around her, but was unable to comfort her.

"*Non mi vedranno mai piu...* They' ll never see me again," she said with calm desperation, "Never again!"

When the children were out of sight, Mr. Castellani walked her to the bedroom and helped her dress. In a few minutes, a car from the Sanitarium arrived.

On November 15, 1937, Mr. Castellani received word that Rosa had died. The following day, she was taken to the Brownstone Funeral Home, in Wilkes Barre, Pennsylvania for a two day wake. The children, especially Rocky, were inconsolable. Seeing their mother in the coffin brought tears to their eyes. When Rocky continued to fix his sight on the face of his mother, his uncle Michael stepped up behind him, picked him up and brought the boy back to the seat.

"Don't be sad, Attilio," Michael said, "your mother has gone to heaven. She will pray for you and for all of us."

"She's in Heaven?"

"Yes, Attilio, she's in Heaven... Don't forget now, you've got to be strong and courageous. You and I have a lot of boxing to do. Is that right?"

Young Rocky looked deep into his uncle's eyes, nodding his head with approval.

On the second day, with the cold weather still bitter, Mrs. Castellani was taken to the church for the finai services. The Italian-speaking priest conducted the rites in front of a small group of relatives and friends.

When the priest finished, everyone lined behind the casket. Young Rocky was first with his father to one side, and then the girls, together with the other relatives and friends for the trip to the Forty Fort Cemetery.

In his isolated little protected world, young Rocky never felt so lost and confused. All of a sudden, the person most dear to him was no longer present. He asked himself what death was and concluded that it was simply the absence of someone, in that case— the absence of his mother. He remembered the days of joy, happiness, of the time his mother had stood up to the mob outside— he, not knowing how sick she really was. In his thoughts, he couldn't believe she was gone, that he would never see her again. It was so unreal. When he asked his father the whereabouts of his mother, Mr. Castellani could only answer that she was in Heaven— *Paradiso*. But that answer did not satisfy young Rocky, not for a long time. Laying on his bed with his eyes staring at the ceiling, he pictured his mother around the house. When tears appeared, he brought his hand to his face to wipe them off— scenes that were to repeat themselves for most of his life.

Although Thanksgiving, Christmas and New Year's went by joylessly, the Castellani were nevertheless able to carry on in spite of the fact that Mr. Castellani was not working at his regular job.

Cousin Michael meanwhile, took more interest in young Rocky, often accompanying him to the gym for their usual workout.

In fifth grade, young Rocky had Mr. Fred L. Shippings as a teacher. Aside from the fact that he liked school very much, Rocky also began to show interest in girls. He was taken by the looks of a cute Polish girl. On Valentine's Day, young Rocky, whose family was still in financial difficulties, watched his classmates exchange commercial Valentine cards, and he not having any, decided to draw one. He did and gave it to the girl. Noticing how well Rocky had drawn it, Mr. Shippings made a big fuss in front of the class. Naturally, Attilio Castellani Jr. felt very proud.

When it came to world affairs, however, Rocky knew very little, as most other children of Italian immigrants. Their problem was survival. Books and newspapers were not necessarily a staple in their households.

"What's going on in the world, these days?" asked Mr. Shippings, who showed a particular interest in current events.

When no one answered, he began to give clues by calling out the name of Hitler.

"I know," said the Polish girl. "I know."

"Well," Mr. Shippings answered encouragingly.

"Hitler is sending his soldiers to fight in other countries. He's trying to start a war in Europe," she remarked.

On seeing her answer as she did, Rocky couldn't help but admire her. At the same time, he felt as though he were stupid.

"That is correct," Mr. Shippings picked up. "Very good. How did you get that information?"

"My dad was listening to the radio. It was also written in the newspapers."

"Very good. Now, who else listened to the radio or read a newspaper or magazine?"

At that question, most of the students put their hands up, except for Rocky, Antonio and few other boys and girls of other ethnic backgrounds.

Attilio, as his teacher called him, was a pretty good student. He liked math and did well enough in other subjects, especially in those where he had to use his visual and motor skills. In current events, except for the fact that his father had once talked about Benito Mussolini attacking Ethiopia, Rocky knew very little. Whenever he had any occasion to listen to any radio, he would always look for a station that carried blow

32

by blow descriptions of boxing matches or baseball games.

During those winter days, when the classrooms were so cold that the teachers complained more than the students about the inefficiency of the coal fired furnaces, there was only one thought in the mind of Rocky— the good weather so he could go outside to play.

When the warmer weather finally came, Rocky quickly began to reactivate the makeshift ring at the abandoned garage, enticing his friends to practice boxing with him. After a while, word got out that young Rocky was too aggressive, that he was beating everyone, and no one wanted to spar or box with him. In seeing with how much passion Rocky followed the sport, some of the kids began to believe that Rocky was obsessed; some even secretly predicted that someday he'd become a champion. Among these were Eddy Chisack, *Goomby* Goombion, Phil Paratore, Gene Machinist and Red. There was also Mary Ann Domblosky. She was the only girl to have beaten Rocky in the makeshift ring, to the glory of the other girls and of the boys who had lost to him; the latter now believed young Rocky was not invincible.

At home, things moved along rather smoothly. Maria and Anna had taken over just about all the chores in the house. Their cooking, too, was generally good, though scarce. Not because they did not know how to cook, but because too often there simply was not that much food to be had. Mr. Castellani always did most of the cooking, scraping as much as he could, but was just unable to bring home enough. Nevertheless, they got along and didn't starve. Mr. Castellani kept the family together; often though, he wondered what they did in the daytime when he was away at work. At supper, he would always ask them what they had done. He was especially curious about his son.

"Attilio, che hai fatto oggi... What did you do

today?"

Rocky, who by now knew exactly what his father was going to ask and when, knew the right answer.

"I stayed around the house, mainly in the yard, picking things up. Then I went to the park to play with the boys."

"What's that I see on your face, under the eye?"

"This?" he said, bringing his hand to the slight bruise under the eye, "Phil and I were doing some fighting and he got me here. It doesn't hurt," he added. The fact was that he had gotten the slight shine from Mary Ann and was too ashamed to admit it. "But I'll get even with her," he said to himself.

By the time Rocky was in sixth grade, Mr. Castellani was working more and more in the mines, having made friends with several co-workers, who helped him out with his English. In one of the colder days of January, there was a serious accident in one of the shafts. Mr. Jugus, who had been a co-worker with Mr. Castellani, died from electrocution after stepping on some exposed wires on the ground. Luck would have it (if the death of a man can be called such), that a group of workers were several feet behind and stopped in time, otherwise many would have been killed alongside Mr. Jugus.

As was the custom, when those tragedies occurred, the members of the various families paid one another home visits. On this occasion, Mr. Castellani brought Rocky along.

Mrs. Jugus was very cordial. She introduced her children— two older sons, Billy and Francis, then her younger daughter Ann, and finally Mary, who was in the sixth grade but in another school. For some reason, Rocky seemed to pay an unusual amount of attention to Mary.

"We're Lithuanians," Mary said, embarrassed by Rocky's stare.

"We're Italians," young Rocky answered.

Pursuant to the great depression of the 30's, the government began to rebuild the neighborhoods. One of these projects was the West Side Settlement House— a type of Y.M.C.A. for the youth of the area. Rocky and his buddies began to frequent the new facilities.

Mr. John Arlington, the boxing coach in charge, was impressed by young Rocky's aggressiveness. In between games of ping pong, basketball and others, Mr. Arlington was even able to arrange some boxing matches for Rocky.

By the end of his sixth grade, Rocky began to need spending money.

"Go shine shoes," advised coach Arlington.

By the time Rocky was finishing sixth grade, he was out on the sidewalks across the river, in the square of downtown Wilkes Barre shining shoes, and doing well. Soon, however, he came across an idea on how to make more money. He devised a system of coupons he himself wrote up. He gave one to each customer who, on returning for the next shine, would receive a discount for as much as a nickel.

During the summer, he became a paper boy, cut grass around the neighborhood and washed cars. When the weather got very hot, he would join his buddies at the local creek on the other side of the Dallas Luzerne Highway. While swimming with his buddies, Phil approached Rocky to tell him that Mary Ann Domblosky was bragging about the fight, and that she was ready for a re-match any time Rocky wanted to.

In the park, there were always kids running around and adults organizing all kinds of games. Rocky had no trouble joining in whatever game was played.

Regardless of what he did in the daytime, he always knew that at a given time, he had to return home, for two reasons: he had to help his sisters with some of the chores; more importantly, he had to be there when his father arrived.

"*Attilio, cosa hai fatto oggi...* What did you do today?" Attilio Sr. asked at the dinner table.

"I shined shoes, sold paper, cut grass and washed cars."

"*Tante cose...* So many things? Very good. At this rate, you're going to be a wealthy man someday. Very good, Attilio. Maria, and you, what did you do?"

One by one, each child answered the father's question. In that way, they kept communication open and stayed close. When Yolanda asked about her mother, Mr. Castellani got a lump in his throat.

"*La mamma...* Mother is in Heaven. Now, let's clear the table..."

"*Attilio, e domani cosa farai...* What are you going to do tomorrow," the father asked?

Rocky paused for a second, not knowing how to answer. His father had never asked questions about the future, always about the past. "Tomorrow?" he answered with hesitation. "I don't know. Maybe the same things," he said. Then he remembered he had a boxing date with Mary Ann. At that moment, he panicked. His faced reddened. "What if she gives me another black eye?" he asked himself.

In bed, he lay awake, thinking of the possible ramifications should Mary Ann beat him again. His eyes staring at the ceiling, he recalled the other match he had had with her, and thought of ways not only to beat her, but to avoid being hit. "How to avoid being hit," he said to himself, as though he had just discovered an important truth about boxing. "Afterall," he thought, "who wants to go through life with a broken nose and scars on the face."

As he pondered, however, he no longer thought of the consequences with his father should he come home with a mark on his face. He felt a certain excitement— an expectation for the coming match, even if it was a girl. She was, afterall, about ten pounds heavier and a couple of inches taller.

Late afternoon the next day, a rather large group of

boys and girls gathered around the makeshift ring in the abandoned garage. Being summer, they all dressed with the oddest clothes (W.P.A.), and some still wore clodhoppers— the heavy three quarter work shoes. The depression wasn't over yet. Many of them, including Rocky, were still feeling its effects. Nevertheless, it didn't dampen the spirits of those kids, most of whom were satisfied to live on bread alone (such is happiness when there is no comparison with better things). They practically lived on dunking bread into coffee.

The many boys and girls took their positions around the ring, the girls mostly to one side cheering, of course, for Mary Ann; scattered among them were some of the boys who obviously cheered for neither fighter— they just liked being close to the girls.

With Phil acting as the referee and Goomby at the bell, the match began. Right from the beginning, Mary Ann had the better of the underweight and smaller kid. Mary Ann punched him and wrestled with him to the girls delight who yelled and screamed when Mary Ann connected. And indeed she did. During the third round, she caught Rocky on the face, right below the eye. But before the fight was over, Rocky was able to even things up. He punched more and avoided being hit, resulting in a wrestling match more than in a boxing match.

With Goomby striking the bell to end the match, Mary Ann, savoring the victory, went to her corner full of smiles. Rocky, who knew he hadn't done well, went to his corner, his head down. Phil got them together in the center of the ring and raised the hand of Mary Ann, to the wild cheers of the girls.

That evening, when Mr. Castellani arrived, Rocky stayed in his room.

"*Dov'è Attilio...* Where is Attilio?" he asked the girls.

"*Sta studiando...* He's studying," Yolanda answered with a snicker.

"Oh!" exclaimed the father, slightly perplexed. Without saying anything else, he went to the bathroom to wash the coal dust off his face. When he returned to the supper table, he found the girls sitting, ready to eat; Rocky was still studying. *"Attilio, vieni a mangiare...* Come to eat," Mr. Castellani ordered with a somewhat loud voice, his face turned in the direction of the door. Then turning to the girls, he suspected something was wrong. *"Ma, che c'è...* What's up?" he asked. Outside of the girls' slight giggling, he got no response. He got his answer, however, when Rocky walked into the kitchen, his face turned to one side. *"Oh, capisco...* I understand," Mr. Castellani commented on seeing his son with a black eye.

"I'm sorry," Rocky said, tears about to run down his face.

"Niente... Nothing, there's nothing to worry about. Just tell me, how did it happen and who did it?"

When his sisters heard those words, and knowing the full story, with smiles on their faces, they looked at their brother. Seeing him embarrassed, they stopped smiling and looked away. With Rocky hesitating, Mr. Castellani interjected. *"Ebbene...* Well then, have you lost your tongue?"

With Rocky more embarrassed, Yolanda finally broke the silence. "He got beaten by a Polish girl."

"Come... What?" Mr. Castellani asked, his forehead wrinkling from the surprise.

"Yes," interrupted Maria, "he got beaten by Mary Ann."

On seeing his son on the verge of tears, he extended his arms and pulled him between his legs. With his arms wrapped around the boy's back, he told him not to cry. At that moment, however, the skinny little Italian kid began to cry. As he sobbed, Mr. Castellani passed his hand over his head and through the young kid's long black hair.

"Ecco, fammi vedere... Here, let me see. You've got

a nice shine, but it isn't too bad. You still look pretty good."

At those words, Rocky took heart. He stopped sobbing. After he wiped his tears from his face, he looked at his father then at his sisters, who were waiting to eat.

"*Va bene. Ora mangiamo...* That's fine. Now let's eat."

Chapter 4

Junior High—Years of Confrontations

In September of 1939, Hitler invaded Poland causing England and France to declare war on Germany. But because there was little if any military activity on the part of the two nations, people began to dub it the *Phony War*. Such was not going to be the case, however, neither for the Europeans nor for the Americans, and especially for families like the Castellani; for, one of the first result of the so-called *Phony War* was the industrial mobilization of America. Suddenly, men who had had a hard time finding jobs, were working 12 to 18 hours a day. And for Mr. Castellani, of course, there was no difference except that those long hours in the coal mines were eventually to have a negative effect on his health.

Seventh grade in Junior High was nevertheless going to be a good year for young Rocky with so many new friends. He had a problem, however, and it had nothing to do with school, which he liked very much. His father, who was working all kinds of hours, had given strict orders that he be in the house with his sisters early in the evening.

Worried about his children being so much alone, Mr. Castellani sought a way to insure they obeyed his order. He knew how easily kids, especially boys, could get in trouble, and waited for the occasion to drive the point home.

One evening, toward the end of September, when the weather was still fair and the people stood outside as long as possible, Rocky, who had been involved with a baseball game that went extra innings, returned home to find, to his surprise, his father waiting at the supper table, with the food on the table still untouched.

"Quali sono i miei ordini... What are my orders!" Mr. Castellani said sternly.

"I was playing baseball..."

"Baseball! I'll give you baseball," he said with a threatening voice. He got up. *"Vieni qua...* Come here," he commanded.

Scared, Rocky moved cautiously toward his father, stopping about two feet from him. At that moment, Mr. Castellani swung his arm wide and caught young Rocky's face with his thick hand, causing the kid to falter to one side. "I'm sorry," Rocky said, as he began to cry. *"Perdonami...* I'm sorry... I won't do it no more," he begged.

"Va bene, questa è l'ultima volta... Promise this is the last time," Mr. Castellani asked sternly.

"Prometto... I promise."

With that, young Rocky moved to his seat, glancing at the terrified expressions of his three sisters, who had been sitting silently. Maria quickly moved to pour water in the glasses and to fill the dishes with lukewarm spaghetti.

In bed, the same evening, Rocky promised himself that he would never again disobey his father. He put his hand over his face. That slap hurt more than any punch he had gotten from anyone. In fact, for the first time in his life, he knew what physical pain really was.

Except for the daytime school activities, Rocky followed a tight schedule the whole of seventh grade. He got along very well at school, and had many more friends than he could ever imagine. He even got closer to *Goomby*— Tom Evans, with whom he had several classes.

Their seventh grade teacher was Mr. Shupmik, who taught Civics and English. The kids liked him very much because he was funny. At times, though, they complained because he gave too much homework. Other times, they thought he was biased.

"What's happening in the world today?" Mr. Shupmik asked.

"There's a war in Europe," answered Lorraine, as usual.

"Who's fighting who?" Mr. Shupmik asked. When Lorraine shot her arm up and began to answer, Mr. Shupmik stopped her. "No, Lorraine. I want to ask someone else. Attilio! Who is fighting who?"

"Hitler," he answered.

"What about Hitler? Where's he from and who else is involved? Tom!"

"Germany," answered Goomby, a smile on his face. He was always the shy but wise guy and the kids enjoyed him.

"Alright," sighed Mr. Shupmik, dissatisfied with one word answers. "Who can tell me a more complete story... Not you Lorraine. I know you know. Well?"

On discovering that few students really knew what was going on, Mr. Shupmik decided to tell them all about it. Thus, he devoted the whole period to Hitler and his rise to power. In particular he chastised France and England for their weakness and predicted that Hitler would take them over. He also chastised the Italians for their venture into Africa. At that point, Rocky became more interested.

"How about the Italians?" Mr. Shupmik asked. "What's their role in all this? Come on Attilio, you should be able to tell me. Aren't you Italian?"

"Ya," answered Rocky.

"Well?"

"I don't know," said young Rocky Castellani.

"Don't your parents talk about what's going on in the world, about Italy?"

"My mother is dead, and my father works the mines. He comes home late. He don't have time."

"He *doesn't* have time, Attilio. Very well, who knows? How about you Antonio?"

Cross eyed as ever, Antonio told the class about *Il Duce,* who was Benito Mussolini, and all the great things *Il Duce* had done for Italy. Surprised, Mr. Shupmik, who opposed Fascism as much as Nazism, challenged Antonio to give facts.

"He built the first Turnpkike in the world. He did away with malaria in many parts of Italy. He built a railroad system..."

"Where the trains run on time?" interrupted Mr. Shupmik.

"Yes, where the trains ran on time," repeated Antonio, to the amazement of the other kids, who admired Antonio for standing up to the teacher.

"Ya," Rocky interrupted.

"What about it, Mr. Castellani, what can you add to what Antonio has said?"

"I don't know nothing about this."

"You don't know *anything* about this. I thought you were Italian and that you speak the language."

"I am... I think I am American, and I speak... I think, Italian," Rocky answered, not sure of himself.

"Well, that's the problem. You're neither Italian nor American. We have to work harder on being Americans— good patriotic Americans, and have to work harder on our English language. The key to success is English; the key to being an American is English, not these other languages."

"Not even French?" interrupted Lorraine. "I'm taking French. It's the language of diplomacy."

"Oh," sighed Mr. Shupmik on being interrupted.

44

"French is fine."

"How about Italian?" asked Antonio, who suddenly became a little brazen.

"And Polish," interrupted Mary Ann, boyish as ever.

"No," Mr. Shupmik answered, "French is a language of international importance. In any event, I don't want to discuss this further. I want to get back to the war in Europe in relationship with America. Because," he said, "that war may very well affect your lives. You may not realize it now... You're so young. But it may well affect your lives."

As far as Rocky was concerned, what was affecting his life was his sister's meals, his father's long work hours, and above all, the absence of the love of his mother. That winter, which was more cold than usual, with snow piling up, they at times wondered if they were going to make it. The war in Europe— the involvement of Italy didn't mean much. Neither his father nor his uncle Michael ever talked about the old country, even though his father spoke Italian. Besides, as far as he was concerned, his only interest was boxing.

Now in High School, Maria began to have problems keeping up with her work. The responsibilities at home were just too much. Although she did not complain to anyone, she was obviously run down. Her homeroom teacher, noticing the difference, talked with Maria's counselor, who in turn called on Maria.

Mrs. Plunket, a veteran of the school, knew exactly how to approach Maria. "Tell me, Maria, it's been a long time since you and I spoke. I know about your mother. Tell me, how are things at home."

"Not too bad," she said unconvincingly.

"Not too bad. What does that mean?"

"Well, I cook and clean the house."

"Do you do all the cooking?"

"My sister helps me a little, and my dad really does most of it."

"You must cook Italian food. You know, I love

Italian food. Do you cook well?" asked Mrs. Plunket.

"Not too good. Sometimes my brother makes fun of me. But he is nice about it. He knows I try."

"What's your favorite dish?"

"Spaghetti!" she said, laughing.

With a smile on her face, Mrs. Plunket said, "Someday, I would like to come visit you. Perhaps you can prepare some *real* spaghetti for me."

"Ya, that would be nice. But our house is not that good."

"I bet it's clean," Mrs. Plunket said.

"Ya, spotless."

"Tell me, Maria, how about school, you seem to be having some difficulty."

"Ya, I guess I'm tired. Besides, I don't understand a lot of things. Math is difficult. English is difficult."

"What can I do to help?"

"I don't know," Maria said.

"What if I got you some help?"

"Great!"

"Maria, how about boys?"

"There is one after me," she said with a proud smile.

"Tell me Maria, is there anything that's really bothering you? After all, you're growing up— practically a woman. Is there anything that's really bothering you?

"Ya, going home and not find our mother there."

By the end of seventh grade, young Rocky had really made a name for himself both in school among his peers and outside on the playing fields and gyms. He won the respect of his friends for his toughness. Whenever anyone made fun of him or of his Italian background, he would take that person into the ring or other suitable places, resulting in teaching them to be more respectful; for himself he gained more confidence to the point that he feared no one. As a matter of fact, he made it known that he would fight anyone at the drop of a hat.

On the last day of school, young Rocky, Phil Paratore, Red, Goomby, Goombion, Eddy Chisack and several other boys as well as Mary Ann and a couple other girls walked across the Kingston Market Street Bridge to Wilkes Barre. While on the bridge, they pulled out their report cards, tore them all in small pieces and threw them down the Susquehanna River, bending over the railing to watch the pieces of paper float away, amidst the boisterous laughter of the boys.

Caddying

At the Irem Temple Golf Course the older boys had created a monopoly on the lucrative jobs. Junior high school boys just didn't have a chance. Again that year word got out that no new boys "need apply" for those jobs.

Rocky had already tried to get into caddying but was rudely denied by those older boys. Feeling confident, he decided to try again.

Word got out that young Rocky and his friends were going to challenge the older boys. These, consequently, under the leadership of a tough-looking high school student, waited for the confrontation, with a certain amount of anxiety. They had heard about Rocky, and somewhere deep inside they felt a little fear which they tried to camouflage by being boisterously united in their commitment to keep all other boys out of the Irem Temple Golf course.

The confrontation came on a warm late afternoon June day, down and away from the main entrance of the course. On seeing Rocky and the other boys, Mike immediately began to sneer at them, calling them different names, including *Pip-Squeak*. When Rocky heard the words *whap* and *black hand*, he became wild. Without fear or emotion, he rammed into Mike, both landing on the ground. With the other boys looking— more or less divided into two sides as

47

though they were witnessing a re-enactment of David and Goliath, Rocky jumped onto his feet, fists held tight in front of him. On seeing Rocky ready to strike, Mike pulled back— for a moment thinking he ought to simply retreat. But because he stood to lose face in front of his buddies, he decided to go on with the match, knowing he was going to lose. He moved forward with his fists up. In a split second, Rocky moved to one side and quickly tagged Mike on the chin with a sharp right, followed by a left that send Mike to the ground.

"Come on, get up," insisted Rocky. "There's plenty more here," he yelled to the cheers of his friends, who kept an eye open in case some of the others had ideas. On seeing Mike remain on the ground, Rocky turned to the others. "Alright, anyone else. Step right in," he said confidently. When no one volunteered, he turned to Mike again. "We're here to work, and we don't want to be told who can work and who cannot. Do you understand?"

At that, Mike got up. "I don't give a damn about the jobs," he blurted, seeing that none of his friends intervened in his behalf.

"One more thing," said Rocky, "I don't wanna ever hear you say those words again, unless you want your head knocked off."

With his caddying job secure, he stopped selling newspapers and shining shoes. Being out there in the open, with so many important people, Rocky felt pretty good. Besides, he got a lot of exercise, made more spending money, and enjoyed it at the same time. The older people liked him, too.

While on the course, he also learned more and more about the world, especially the war situation in Europe, from the various players who, for the most part, were obviously affluent and educated. He learned, for instance, that a Nazi Panzer Division ripped through French defenses— the impermeable Maginot

Line— with unheard of speed, resulting in France's surrender. He also learned, mostly from golfers of Jewish background, about Hitler's sweep into Greece, Crete, North Africa, etc. He even heard awful words about Jews getting killed just because they were Jews— which was the thing he understood the least.

With these thoughts in mind, Rocky and his buddies began to think more and more about the war, scheming on how to enlist against Hitler. Rocky's interest in boxing, however, was still uppermost in his mind. He began to think that maybe he might be able to start boxing on a regular basis, and that he should change his name. At time, because he feared his father, he also thought of changing his name to Costello in anticipation of fighting for money, as he would do very shortly. After several attempts at different names, and while daydreaming of going to war, he finally settled on *Roxy Wargo,* for his future professional career— (*Roxy* symbolized his mother Rose, and *Wargo* going to war).

He continued to go to the settlement house in Pringle, always seeking out Mr. Arlington, who ran a tight ship, taking no lip from anyone. Rocky, who had been exposed to a rigid code by his father, didn't mind Mr. Arlington's stringent guidelines.

"Good morning sir," Rocky greeted Mr. Arlington, knowing how much the coach liked to be respected.

"Hello Attilio," Mr. Arlington answered, a smile on his face, obviously happy to see the young boy, and as happy about the boy's greeting. "Come on, get ready, we'll show you a few tricks in boxing today."

After a good workout, wherein Rocky was sweating profusely, Mr. Arlington told him that he had a boy to match him with for the up-coming Catholic Youth Centers sponsorship which was under his guidance. Mr. Arlington arranged for Rocky to fight. Thusly, young Rocky Castellani was informed of the up-coming championship fights to be held by the Catholic Youth Center.

Excited, Rocky nevertheless kept it a secret, not telling his sisters nor his father. One evening, having been detained at a friend's house where he listened to a baseball game on the radio, he forgot his curfew. Finally realizing he was late, he rushed home only to find his father waiting, as once before, at the dinner table. This time, though, he didn't know what to expect, wondering if his father might have gotten word about the boxing tournament, and the fact that he had agreed without his father's consent.

"Dove sei stato... Where were you?" Mr. Castellani asked in his usual firm way.

"A casa di un amico... At the home of a friend, listening to the baseball game. I'm sorry I'm late."

"Va bene... All right! We'll let it go this time. Go wash up."

Somehow, Mr. Castellani sensed something was not right with his children. Rocky was now 14 years old and could see his son becoming more and more independent, secretly marveling at Rocky's build— like that of a fighter, he thought. With the girls, however, things also seemed different; yet, he couldn't figure out exactly what was happening. He saw that Maria was changing— she was now seventeen.

Secretly, Maria had been seeing a young man by the name of Bill. She was finding her senior year too difficult. When Bill asked her to get married, she quickly accepted.

"Che vuoi fare... What can you do?" said Mr. Castellani to his brother Mike Castellani, who was visiting at the house.

"But she's so young?"

"And has only this year to go," Mr. Castellani commented in a sad tone of voice.

"Are you going to approve?" Mike Castellani asked.

"What else can I do?" said Attilio Sr.

Having had her father's blessing, Maria immediately made the necessary arrangements, and in two month's time, she would be marrying Bill, a sheetmetal worker from New Jersey.

With the help of uncle Mike, Maria got the local hall for ten dollars. Because there was no Catholic Church in Luzerne, she arranged to be married at St. Anna's Catholic Church in Wilkes Barre.

The church ceremony was very simple, with only the immediate members of the families present. At the hall, there was plenty to eat. And of course, there was dancing to a trio which specialized in typical Italian and Neapolitan songs. For obvious reasons, however, Rocky seemed to have gotten most of the attention, for he was always surrounded by the younger kids who followed him wherever he went.

With Maria gone to live with her husband in New Jersey, the Castellani had to make another adjustment. This time, it was not as bad as the first when Mrs. Castellani died, and it wasn't clear that Anna could take over.

The First Championship

With the C.Y.C. having made all preparations for the boxing tournament, Rocky waited and trained for the event as though nothing else existed in the world. He established a regimen for himself— something very unusual for a young man, and stayed with it. When he was away from the makeshift ring, or from the gym or parks, he would do shadow boxing at home, in front of the mirror, being sure no one saw him, especially his father. He hadn't said anything to anyone except for his uncle Michael from whom he extracted a promise of secrecy.

The C.Y.C. championship fights were held Saturday night, with each challenger patiently sitting and waiting his turn for his next match. Uncle Michael was in the crowd.

Rocky's first match started at 7:30, winning it without much difficulty. The second match began at 8:44, and that was much more difficult. It turned out to be a slug match with an awful lot of hard hitting, being one of the longest and worse fights he had had up to that time.

He was spitting blood when at 11:05 he was called out for his third match. Weighing at 105 pounds, he wobbled his way to the ring to the wild cheers of the crowd, and of his uncle Michael. When the other boxer appeared, there were also cheers, but not as many as for Rocky. Though he was pleased by the reception, he nevertheless was anxious. What he did not know was that his opponent was as tired as he was.

The fight went the full three rounds. Although it was not the greatest of matches, Rocky was able to outpoint and out punch his tired opponent, resulting in an unanimous decision on behalf of young Rocky, and therefore, his first championship.

Early next morning, those who participated in the tournament gathered at St. Mary's Church for the early Mass. The winners sat in the first row, with all others in the back rows. Anna and Yolanda sat in the rear, excited over what was happening— Rocky this time just couldn't keep the secret from them and had asked them to be present.

When the Priest proclaimed the various champions, the girls smiled with pride when Rocky's name was called out. Uncle Michael unexpectedly began to clap, causing the others to follow suit.

Because he now had various opportunities to fight for money and prizes, young Rocky adopted his uncle Michael's last name, calling himself Billy Costello.

In 1941, Hitler attacked Russia. The United States, meantime, cautiously watched the goings on in the world, uneasy over its isolationistic stance. Too many people, however, including many politicians, saw the handwriting on the wall. Uppermost in their minds was which side to choose. Many, consciously or otherwise, began to take sides. The Americans of

Italian descent, while Mussolini stayed neutral, supported Italy for the most part, many contributing money and gold chains to the Fascist government. The Americans of German descent did likewise on behalf of Nazi Germany. Except for groups of people in Hollywood and others belonging to the intelligentsia that supported the Soviet Union, most Americans initially seemed to have a pre-disposition toward Germany and Italy. They admired the two leaders for the changes they had brought about in their countries, liking especially the new but controlled social order and the industrial progress. Few, including American Jews, cared much of what was happening to the European Jews in Germany. As for Japan, fears over that country's militarization was worrying only top U.S. military brass.

While Europe was ablaze with Hitler's deadly war machine, many Americans enjoyed life as best they could. At the Irem Temple Country Club, its members continued with their sports and social activities, their peace and tranquillity threatened only by their caddies fighting over their turf.

With Rocky more or less the unchosen leader, he was now in the position to protect his job and that of his buddies. There was an unwritten law the local boys relished, and it was that no outsiders could come in. During an assignment of positions, Jack Crossig, the man in charge, gave a slot to caddy first to a boy over the objection of another who pretended that slot. One thing led to another. Finally, for some unexplainable reason, a whole bunch of them gathered around the thirteenth hole where they began to push and shove one another. In no time, they were wrestling and fighting. Rocky, naturally, was at the center of the brawl doing his thing with his fists against Jack. With Phil to one side and Goomby on the other, Rocky did well defending himself. Suddenly, a boy rushed forward and landed a stinging solid punch on Rocky's nose, knocking him to the ground. His hand over the nose, Rocky felt groggy. In a couple of seconds, blood began to flow from his nose.

On seeing the caddies fighting, several golfers converged on them. With a certain amount of effort, they succeeded in breaking up the bloody brawl. Of all the boys, Rocky was most thankful for the timely interference.

For the Irem Temple Country Club members, and those few golfers on the thirteenth, that probably was the closest they had come to witnessing or participating in a battle. Deep in their hearts, however, that battle may have been foreboding.

Chapter 5

Love of Sports

Although ninth grade was housed in the junior high, for all practical purposes it belonged to the high school curriculum which required four years.

Mrs. Henderson, the high school nurse, was amazed to discover how healthy Rocky was. She knew the history of his family and was very much aware that Rocky and his sisters had been living at the poverty level since Mr. Castellani had immigrated to the United States. Mrs. Henderson also knew the death of Mrs. Castellani had created additional hardships on the children's nutrition. Yet, in spite of it all, Rocky was healthy and strong.

Ninth grade turned out to be a troublesome year for Rocky; he became mischievous and rambunctious. Together with Gene and Mark Machinist, Rocky created a little bit of hell both with Mrs. Henderson, his homeroom teacher, and with Miss. Marrian Marcin, his English teacher. However, he knew just how far he could go. As a result, he never had to go to the office for punishment. His teachers were aware of the fact that young Rocky was becoming popular with sports and getting all kind of attention. They also saw the attention had gone to his head. Their challenge, therefore, was to keep Rocky out of trouble so he could have a viable year. Among themselves, they wondered how long Rocky would remain in school, knowing about Maria, and about Mr. Castellani, who had become despondent and erratic in his behavior toward his children.

Rocky spent a lot of time with uncle Michael, going to his house to listen to boxing matches on the radio. Rocky was particularly interested in the world middle-weight championship fight between George Abrams and Tony Zale. Both Michael and Rocky favored Zale, who won the fifteen round bout by decision.

On going to church, the Sunday after Thanksgiving, Rocky, Anna and Yolanda, learned that America was at war— Japan had bombed Pearl Harbor in Hawaii. As a result, the United States declared war on both Germany and Japan. During Mass, the priest talked at length about the world situation. Although his sermon had a pessimistic tone, except for the older parishioners who remembered the First World War, not too many others shared in that pessimism. Rocky, of course, did not understand any of it; nor did he think the war was going to affect him at that moment. The only thing which bothered him was the fact that his father was not at home on a regular basis, that too often, he was left alone for extended periods of time with his two sisters.

On arriving home from a New Year's Eve party at about 1:30 AM, Rocky and Anna got worried when they found the door locked. Their father apparently had already gotten back, and they were afraid he would punish them. When they finally succeeded in opening the back door and got into the kitchen, there they saw Mr. Castellani waiting. Without saying a word, however, he turned and went to his room upstairs, leaving the kids dumfounded and confused.

Basketball

The West Side Settlement House in Pringle offered many sports activities for the young kids. In the 1942-43 season, young Rocky got a Certificate of Award for his participation in Spring Basketball, signed by Mrs. Mary Ann Thurston and by Mr. Russell T. Williams, Principal and Director of Athletics. But the man Rocky liked the most was Father Dolan. A friend to all the kids, Father Dolan took a special liking to Rocky. He followed Attilio's budding career very closely, counseling him and helping him in more ways than one, even in private matters. This Priest of Irish descent certainly had a positive and meaningful impact on young people.

In one of the games, Rocky was involved in a brawl with Lenny Urban of the other team. With friends like Mark Gushanas, Phil Paratore, Goomby, Gommbian, Red, Eddy and many others present, Rocky played the game as though it was the last game left in the world, blocking Lenny in every way possible. Angry and exasperated by Rocky's successful blocks, Lenny attempted to steam roll over young Rocky. With the score tied, Lenny desperately tried again. But Rocky proved once again the stumbling block. Infuriated, Lenny grabbed the ball, aimed it right at Rocky's face and threw it with all his might. On seeing it coming, Rocky ducked, stumbling to the floor. He immediately got up and ran after Lenny. He grabbed him and proceeded to give him a beating, much to the satisfaction of the crowd which cheered Rocky on. Rocky, however, did not come out of the fight without bruises. Father Dolan and Mr. Williams finally broke up the fight, thus saving the two combatants additional bumps.

With the war raging in the world, the teachers could not help talk about those events. Somehow, they felt that their kids, who were between fourteen and sixteen, would soon become involved in the tragic war, which had already brought about half day sessions.

"Who's Stalin?" Miss. Marcin asked in her English class.

Naturally, Lorraine put her hand up. But like the teachers of the past grades, Miss. Marcin avoided Lorraine. Instead, she called on another student. When the student stumbled for the answer, Lorraine shot her hand up again. "I know, I know," she said eagerly.

"Very well, then, being that no one knows or cares to tell," she said, and recognized Lorraine.

"Stalin is a dictator in Russia. He took over after the Revolution. He is responsible for the murder of millions of people..."

"Wait a second," interrupted Miss. Marcin, "who told you that?"

"My father! He shows me the papers he gets and I read them."

"Millions of people!" whispered Rocky to Antonio. "What's she talking about?"

"Attilio, do you have a question?" asked Miss. Marcin.

"No!" he said quietly.

Although he finished ninth grade and was now fifteen years old, Rocky continued caddying for the summer. However, what he was making was not enough to cover his expenses. Besides, he was participating with the up-keep of the family.

When he returned to school that September, he felt his heart was somewhere else. He daydreamed about boxing, creating all kinds of fantasies around becoming Roxy Wargo and winning a world boxing championship. He even began to talk about this to his friends, who, after a while, became bored.

Chapter 6

Family, High School, Boxing

Because of the war, the Luzerne County School System continued with half sessions. Rocky was lucky enough to go to the morning session, thus having enough free time to work and to keep physically fit.

For some reason, Rocky had a tough time in school. His lack of enthusiasm for books and for learning in general was very evident, causing his teachers to be concerned. Even Father Dolan, on learning about Rocky's disinterest, took him aside.

"I don't know, Father Dolan," Rocky answered. "Somehow, since my mother died, it seems nothing is going right at home. We try, but things are not the same. My father has a lot of trouble. And my sisters too. I do the best I can, but you know, many times we don't even have enough to eat. We ate more when we were poorer, when my mother was around, than now that we have a little more. But I am worried about my father. I just wish he finds someone, you know, another woman. It's been a while since my mother died."

"I know, Attilio. It is always more difficult to replace a mother than a father. Mothers should simply never go. In your situation, God took her and there is nothing anyone can do. We have to do the best we can. The thing to remember is that she just didn't pick up and go."

"I know, I know."

"But Attilio, how about school? What's happening with school?"

"Nothing. I'm just bored. I don't like it at all. Besides, I don't understand many things and I don't care to learn them. Some of those things are stupid, especially math problems. I can't even read the English let alone solve the problems."

"But Attilio," Father Dolan said in a soft and affectionate tone. "We can get help for you. I want you to be successful at school. These days, you know, a high school diploma is very important. You don't want to work the mines like your father, do you?"

"No, I want to be a boxer," the young boy answered.

"Even a boxer, you've got to be an intelligent one, one with at least a high school diploma."

"I know," answered Rocky in a subdued voice, realizing Father Dolan had understood about his intentions to quit school. I'll keep trying. I'll do my best."

"Good, that's what I like to hear. By the way, what are you all doing for the coming holy days?"

"Oh, nothing unusual. We'll stay at home, have our usual dinner— nothing special, you know, and then we'll go to different places. I may go to uncle Mike's with my sisters. I don't know."

Christmas and the New Year did arrive. As young Rocky Castellani predicted, there was no family spirit. His father was home, but only physically, and his sisters tried to do the best they could with their various little gifts. Certainly, with the mother not being there, no matter how many more material things they might have had, the holidays simply were not the same— the emptiness was overwhelming.

The Castellani family spent Christmas day with uncle Michael Castellani Sr., whose family did their best to entertain, preparing the usual Italian dinner, with plenty of pasta, meat, salads and desserts. Michael took care of the wine, being sure to have a robust red for the adults and a milder white wine for the women and children.

After the long dinner, the men and boys gathered around in the living room to listen to the radio, and to talk about sports. The conversation, however, turned to boxing: who were the various champions in the various categories, and what Italian names held what titles, and who were the runners-up. Although Michael Jr. did most of the talking, Mr. Castellani was surprised to see how much his son Rocky knew about the sport. Attilio Sr. tried to inject himself in the conversation, but couldn't for the reason that he didn't know much about the sport, but really because his mind and heart were elsewhere. He thought about his wife, and about this woman with whom he was spending time. While his son was engrossed in the conversation, Mr. Castellani thought about the day when he would be bringing her home, wondering about his kids' reactions.

A couple of weeks later, Rocky nonchalantly stopped going to school, without saying anything to his father or sisters. Noticing Rocky was not going to school, Mr. Castellani offered to get him a full time job in the mines. Not having much choice, as there were no other jobs, Rocky acceded.

For that entire year, Rocky worked along side his father, in those cold and dark mines, full of black soot which impregnated his clothes and skin. It didn't take long for Rocky to decide that mining coal was not for him. Nevertheless, he stayed on, partially to make his father happy, partially because at least he was not on the streets bumming around, and because of the money he was making, though it wasn't much. Throughout this period of hard work, unbeknown to him, Rocky gained endurance. His long hours of pick and shovel, though not doing him much psychologically, affected him physiologically. In his constant training after work and during weekends, he could feel there was a difference in his physical strength and abilities. His friends at the gym as well as his uncle Michael had noticed the difference.

"Hey Attilio," said his uncle, who had just arrived at the gym from work. "Rocky, get those filthy clothes off, will you! I wanna' talk to you."

Rocky took off his clothes. As he was about to go to the shower, his uncle began to laugh aloud.

"What's the matter?" young Rocky asked.

"What's the matter?" Michael repeated. "You're like a *bedouin*. You're black all over. If I didn't know you, I'd swear you were black."

"Come on, uncle Mike. It's not that bad."

During a short morning break, deep in the mine whose black coal at times reflected bizarre shades of vermilion colors according to the angle of the light, Mr. Castellani sat to one side with his son. He was in a deep pensive mood, more reflective than he had ever been before. Rocky, who had noticed his father's brooding, did not question him in any way, though he was secretely worried. His working the mine along side his father taught him to appreciate the inhuman sacrifice of his immigrant father.

"*Vedi, in queste miniere...* See, in these mines, we all get destroyed, sooner or later. Either we die like my friend, Jugus..."

"You mean Mary's father," interrupted Rocky, surprising his father.

"*Si...* Yes, like Mr. Jugus, or like so many others who get sick— miner's disease! You've heard of it."

"*Lo so...* I know it. A lot of miners die," Rocky said.

"*Ma io non voglio...* But I, I don't want you to die like the rest of us. Do you understand!"

"Yes, but, what else can I do? There are no jobs," Rocky complained as he crossed his forehead with the back of his hand, leaving streaks of colorful shiny lines on his white skin. "The only thing I can do is fight."

"*Non mi piace...* I don't like it, but if that will get you out of this miserable place— I don't even feel like a human being here— then go ahead."

Rocky looked at his dejected father, who seemed smaller than he actually was. At times, Mr. Castellani seemed to disappear in the coal itself. With his clothes being black, except for the helmet which practically covered his whole head, Mr. Castellani was subdued even in his voice.

"*Papa...* Dad, what can I do to help. Why don't you get another job?"

"What job? *Io non so fare niente...* I can't do anything else. In Italy at least I could work the farm and scrounge a living. Here, I have to scrounge a living from these mines. Thank God for these mines, otherwise we would all be starving— not that we have been eating that well," the elder Castellani said.

While they talked, a voice from a short distance away ordered them back to work. Lazily, the two got up, picked up their tools, and moved to their area of work.

In order to make a few more dollars so he could quit the mines, Rocky agreed to fight whenever he could. Calling himself Billy Costello, he agreed to fight on the following conditions: one dollar if he lost, two dollars or a wristwatch if he won. For the next several months, he fought a lot and made a little more money, but not enough to justify his quitting the mines. Finally, toward the year end, just before the holidays, on a cold Saturday morning, young Rocky, who was downtown with several of his buddies, got an offer to fight for twenty dollars.

"Hey," this stranger said, on coming out of a restaurant. "Any of you wanna fight? There's 20 bucks in it," he added. The man was different looking, but obviously serious in his proposition. Rocky was amazed at the 20 dollar figure, knowing he was making 35 cents an hour.

"Fight!" Phil Paratore exclaimed. "What do you have in mind?"

At that point, the man explained he needed someone to go with him to Scranton, Pennsylvania where he had made arrangements for a bout at the famous Wattras Armory, but that one of the boxers had gotten ill.

Phil, who had done the initial talking, turned to Rocky, as did his other friends. "It's all yours, Attilio."

He looked at the man, suspiciously. "Is this on the up and up?"

"Yeh, kid, of course it is. I'm a promoter."

"How would I get there. I have no car," young Rocky said.

"Don't worry. I have a car. I'll take you there and take you back. Transportation is no problem."

With that, Rocky agreed, provided he could go home to get his equipment. When he got home, he found his sisters and father eating in the kitchen. Without saying anything as to where he was going, he left to join the man with the big car.

At the Wattras Armory, suddenly Rocky realized that if he used his uncle's name, his father might find out. Besides, his uncle was in the Armory. In that instant, when asked his name, he answered, "Wargo, Roxy Wargo."

Being he did not have a license to fight, the promoter quickly made the arrangement, and Rocky got his first license to fight his first bonafide match of four rounds. He was in good shape and anxious to show his stuff. On entering the ring, in that strange place full of people, he felt dejected when no one cheered. His head bolted back on hearing the crowd cheer his opponent. At that point, the promoter approached Rocky.

"I want you to lose," he said, looking at Rocky squarely in the eyes. "Lose, hear me!" he repeated with emphasis.

Rocky did not answer. "So this is the world of professional boxing?" he asked himself, knowing the only way he was going to lose was to be beaten.

"Well, kid!" the man blurted on seeing Rocky not responding.

"You asked me to fight, and I agreed to it," Rocky answered matter of fact.

"Lose, I told you," threatened the man.

"Attilio," Mike cried out, leaning through the ropes, his hands cupping his mouth, "You better win, boy; I got money bet on you, hear?"

With those words, Rocky was no longer sure about his conviction to fight to win or lose. The promoter gave one last glare and stepped aside. Rocky, alone in his corner, with the opponent in the other corner, suddenly felt insecure and weak. He looked at Mike and back to the disappearing promoter. Alone he sought a way out, but his mind simply did not work so fast. Then, in a split second, he had the idea that by fighting to a draw, he would satisfy every one.

After the referee gave each fighter the appropriate instructions, the match began with a fury of punches, Rocky being sure that for every punch he received, he gave one back, and for every hold there was one in return. With the fight progressing more or less evenly, Michael kept on yelling at Rocky to use his left hook, then a right to the head and so on. Rocky could hear his uncle cheer; he could also see the nameless promoter in the corner, analyzing all that was going on, and not necessarily happy about what was happening. Nevertheless, the match went as planned. When it was over, the judges decided on a draw, a decision that displeased every one, especially his uncle. With his head down, he wondered what to say to the promoter and to his uncle. Finally, he decided not to discuss the match at all. He just picked up his money and arranged with his uncle to return home.

On entering the house, he found his sisters together

with a woman in the kitchen. Mr. Castellani was in his bedroom.

"Yolanda, I'm home," he said with a great big smile on his face. Then, becoming serious, he turned toward the rather chubby short woman. "Hi, my name's Attilio."

Anna quickly interrupted. "Attilio, this is Marianna. She's pop's friend."

"Oh," said Rocky. "Where's pop?" he asked as he eyed the woman, un-impressed by her demeanor.

"He'll be right back. I'll heat the coffee," Anna said.

"Attilio," interrupted Yolanda, "I see you got hit in the face. I hope it doesn't hurt much. You were fighting, huh?"

"How are you? I heard a lot about you," Marianna said to Rocky. Noticing the boy was somewhat cold, she added, "Your father tells me you're a good boy."

"Ya, I know."

Mr. Castellani eyed Rocky to study his reactions regarding Marianna; they sat around the kitchen table eating and drinking strong espresso that Anna had reheated with the old Neapolitan coffee pot. Rocky kept watching Marianna eat. When she went for more food, he pulled the plate away, saying he needed to save some later. Mr. Castellani looked at his son but did not say anything. His son's message was clear— he did not like her.

Later that evening, when Rocky was alone with his two sisters, he began to ask questions about the woman. On seeing neither Yolanda nor Anna knew much, he asked for their opinion.

"I don't know," answered Yolanda, winking her eye.

"She seems nice," added Anna from the sink where she was washing the dishes and placing them up on the shelf to dry along side the various utensils including the knives, forks and spoons.

"She seems mean. I don't know if I like her," Rocky commented pensively. "I don't know. But, if she's what Papa wants, I guess we will have to go along with him. By the way, did you see how she ate! I thought she was never going to stop."

"Ya!" commented Yolanda, always the first to talk.

"In any event, I don't think Papa is too well. You girls have to keep an eye on him... By the way— and don't say anything to him— I'm getting more and more into boxing."

"Ya, I know," Lonnie said, wondering why they hadn't said anything about her brother's face.

"I'm fighting under the name of Roxy Wargo."

"*Roxy!*" exclaimed Yolanda. "What kind of a name is that? *Roxy?*"

"Ya, Roxy, and one day I'm gonna be a champion!" he said, and went on to explain how he had gotten the name of *Wargo.*

Rocky had chosen the name of Billy Costello, after his uncle Michael Castellani Jr.— his real name was Michael Costello Jr. given him by the midwife who had made a mistake on the birth certificate. When Attilio Sr. showed suspicion, Rocky changed from Billy Costello to Roxy Wargo.

For some un-explainable reason, Rocky just did not take to Marianna. He thought about her, but could not find much to like. In any event, as he had told himself before, out of respect for his father, he was going to do his best to be friendly. However, things were not going to be smooth, and he knew he would have to make a special effort to be nice.

About two weeks later, after winning a convincing four round match, he brought home a box of doughnuts to celebrate the victory. On entering, he found Yolanda and Anna in the living room, and Marianna in the kitchen.

When Rocky appeared with the box, Yolanda rushed to wrap her arms around him. "Attilio!" she exclaimed, "you got doughnuts!"

On hearing Yolanda, Marianna stepped into the living room and asked Rocky if he would share the doughnuts with them. Begrudgingly, Rocky agreed and walked to the kitchen. Yolanda, however, beat her brother to the door by stepping in front.

With Marianna seated at the table, Anna made the usual espresso coffee. Rocky, meanwhile, made sure to keep the box closed, opening it only when the coffee was ready and dispersing one doughnut at a time.

"May I have another," asked Marianna.

"I think you've had enough," Rocky answered sternly.

"Oh, come on, Attilio, let her have another," Yolanda interjected pleadingly.

"You think you a' tough," Marianna commented in broken English, her mimicking rather obvious.

"No!" Rocky answered in a rude voice. "Look how fat she is. She don't need another doughnut."

"You take that back," charged Marianna angrily, her face red.

"I ain't tak'n nothing back," young Rocky answered.

Marianna extended her hand, grabbed a doughnut and brought it to her mouth. She took a deep bite and put the rest back in the box. "You eat the rest," she told Rocky authoritatively.

On seeing Rocky glare at her, she got up, walked to the kitchen sink, picked up one of the larger knives and returned to the table. Placing the point to Rocky's throat, she commanded him to eat the rest. At that unexpected sight, Anna began to scream; Yolanda was terrified and started to tell Marianna to pull back.

"No!" she yelled, the knife touching Rocky's skin. "You eat it now or else."

"OK! OK!" Rocky answered when he felt the point of the knife. "Just put the knife away."

"No, first you eat the doughnut," she insisted.

At that point, with his sisters terrified, Rocky decided not to take any chances. He slowly extended his hand, picked it up and put it to his mouth. "Now, pull back," he asked.

"No!", she answered vehemently. "First you eat it."

With that, Rocky took a first bite on the opposite side of her bite. Finally, he ate the whole doughnut, quickly burping as though he had just swallowed a lump. "Now, pull back," he asked.

When Marianna pulled back, the girls were relieved. They watched the woman swagger to the sink to put back the knife. Rocky got up, powder sugar still on his mouth. When Marianna turned to go back to her chair, Rocky extended his powerful arm and caught her on the forehead with a huge punch, knocking her to the floor. The girls screamed. On seeing Marianna not moving, they rushed to her.

"She's dead!" Yolanda yelled as she bent down to help Marianna.

"She ain't dead," Rocky commented nervously. He bent to check her out.

"She's dead! She dead!" Yolanda screamed desperately while Anna tried to revive Marianna.

On seeing the woman not moving, Rocky became concerned.

"Run, run away!" Yolanda yelled.

Terror stricken, Rocky rushed to his bedroom, picked up some things and rushed out the house: The two girls, helpless and in tears, began to wipe Marianna's face with a wet cloth. When they saw the woman still not moving, they began to invoke the name of the Madonna, their eyes turning toward the ceiling.

"Oh, Mamma mia, what can we do?" Yolanda pleaded invokingly.

After about a minute, Marianna moved her arm and began to moan. Yolanda's eyes brightened; Anna immediately took her hand and began to rub it.

"Oh, God," Marianna moaned. "What happened!" she began to ask, as she was coming to.

After a couple of minutes, with her hand covering her forehead, she remembered Rocky's punch.

"That idiot," she blurted angrily. "He'll pay for this, that animal!"

At those words, the girls froze. Pulling away, they sat on their chairs without saying a word, watching Marianna getting up slowly and moving to her chair.

Just as the three women began to relax, Mr. Castellani returned. On finding Marianna with her bruised forehead, he quickly became alarmed and asked what had happened.

"Attilio hit her," Yolanda said.

"Ya, but..." interrupted Anna, who wanted to explain about the knife.

"That moron, he'll pay for it," blurted Marianna. "Take me home," she commanded. "I'm gonna call the cops!"

"*Va bene...* Fine," he consented.

"*Va bene, va ben,*" she repeated mockingly. "We're in America now. Can't you speak *da English?*" she angrily blurted once again.

"*Ho capito...* I understand," he said in a subdued voice. "I understand. Come on, I'll take you home." He put his hand under her arm and helped her up. "*Dov'è Attilio...* Where's Attilio?" he asked Anna.

"*Non lo so...* I don't know."

"He ran away," added Yolanda.

"You cannot call the cops, you can't," said Mr. Castellani.

"Oh, yeah?" Marianna blurted, "just watch me!"

On hearing that their brother might go to jail the two sisters began to cry, "Attilio, Attilio!"

When Mr. Castellani got back home, he found the girls sleeping in bed. He then sat in the dimly lit living room. "*Madonna mia, questa è l'America. Mannaggia!...* Mother of God, this is America. Damned!"

With a heavy heart and worried, Rocky walked a few miles then started to hitch hike out of the Wyoming Valley to New Jersey, with the hope of staying at his sister's place until the thing blew over. After about twelve hours on the road, he reached his sister at noon the next day, only to find that the State

Police had been there earlier to ask about him. Marianna, who had gone to the hospital to check her forehead, made a report to the police. However, being that she felt better the next morning, and because Mr. Castellani begged her to call the whole thing off, especially because she had caused the incident, she finally did agree.

On seeing Maria, Rocky put his long and powerful arms around her hugging her gently but firmly. With tears in his eyes, he told her what had happened, asking her to let him stay with her for a short period of time. When she told him the police had been there, he got worried.

"My God, where can I go now?" he asked, his eyes cast on the floor.

"No where. You stay here now. I'll cook you something first. Then you rest, 'cause I see you're tired. Then we'll see. We'll decide when my husband comes home from work tonight."

Maria took her brother to the small kitchen. After sitting him down and apologizing for the kind of apartment she had, she began to make a pepper omelet. "I got some Italian bread this morning. See what a nice *panella.*"

Rocky picked up the large loaf of fresh bread and began to slice a piece with the knife, his eyes on the shiny blade.

"Che buono... How good!" he exclaimed, as he bit hard into the crunchy crust.

"You still speak Italian, eh!" Maria commented with a smile.

"I guess so, though I don't talk much anymore," said Rocky.

After having eaten the large omelet and consumed practically half the loaf, he went to the couch, layed down and slept till his brother-in-law Bill arrived.

With Maria briefing her husband, the two decided the best thing for the 16 year old kid would be to go back home and face charges.

"We don't want you to have a record," said Maria. "Tomorrow morning you go home and report to the police right away."

"Sure," Rocky answered. He looked at his brother-in-law and understood they had already talked about this. "Sure," he repeated. "I guess I have no choice."

Early morning, after hugging Maria and given a solid hand shake to his brother-in-law, Rocky left town to begin hitch-hiking back. By evening, he reached Luzerne. As he started to go toward his house, he suddenly changed his mind and decided to go to his uncle's house. Walking by a Recruitment Poster of the U.S.M.C., he paused momentarily, but continued on. He was too preoccupied with what lay ahead.

Michael and his wife had heard about the incident and knew the police wanted to talk to him. When the kid appeared at the door, Michael was both surprised and relieved.

"Where have you been?" he asked, happy to see his cousin. "Come on in; we gotta talk about a lot of things."

Inside, uncle Michael immediately put Rocky at ease. The wife told Rocky to stay for supper. When Mr. Costello suggested Rocky hide in the attic until they figured something out, Mrs. Costello agreed.

Immediately after supper, Michael rushed over to see Mr. Castellani, who was home with Yolanda and Anna.

"Senti, Attilio... Listen, Attilio, I know all that happened, and I am very much worried about Rocky. You know, the woman was wrong. We can't let the kid have a record, you know that."

"Lo so... I know Michael. There won't be a record. I spoke with her and she agreed to drop the whole thing."

"Good, now he can come home. You know, he's over my house. I'll have him come home tomorrow."

"Va bene... That is fine. Tell him not to worry. He's a good kid; he means well. Just that this America at

times is hard to understand. So many crazy things, so many crazy people. At times I feel like going back to the old country."

Michael Jr. went home and told his father all that had happened. As a result, Michael Sr. immediately went to visit Mr. Castellani to see how he could be of help.

"I understand how you feel, Attilio. But we have to have patience. Remember, we came here with nothing. We didn't even have a language. Look at the two of us. We speak with each other in Italian— not in our dialect. Why, because we come from the South and some from the *Middle*. Our dialects are different. So we speak in Italian as best we can because we never went to school to really learn it. What did you do, third grade? Me, I didn't even do second grade. Beside, when we came here, we couldn't learn English. This language is too hard. We'll die here and never learn the language. But our kids do, and they will go on. Problem is that they soon forget even the few words of dialect they learn from us. You see, Attilio, I've been noticing that soon or later, we won't be able to even speak with our kids," said Mike.

"That's the problem I'm having. It seems we don't talk no more. I'm having problems even with my girls. If their mother had been here, maybe things would have been different. I think of getting another woman, and you know what happened."

"Well, don't worry. Things will straighten out," Mike said.

"Beviamo un po di vino... About having some wine?"

"Great! But no more talk about the old country. Remember, it never gave us much. Not even the church helped us. It didn't help us there; it ain't helping us here. We go to the basement of the Irish church to hear Mass, and that's all. The few priests that speak Italian don't count much."

"Salute... To our health," he said, bringing up his

73

glass of wine and touching his brother's glass.

"*Alla nostra salute*... To our health and that of our children. We have nothing else," he added in a serious tone.

After drinking their wine, Michael gave his brother a hug and went back home with the good news.

Chapter 7

Falsifying the Birth Certificate

Next morning, being Saturday and everyone was home, Mrs. Costello prepared a hearty breakfast: fried eggs in olive oil, fresh Italian bread— round loaf, and espresso coffee with warm milk. With his little cousins swarming around him, Rocky felt pretty good especially over the news his cousin had brought him. Now, however, he had something else on his mind. During the night, he had a hard time sleeping, worrying over the police and over that woman. Not having a solution, he decided to check out the local recruiting office and see if he could join the marines as a way out of his predicament.

"Uncle Michael," Rocky said, pushing a piece of bread into the yoke of the egg, "I think I wanna join the marines."

"What!" exclaimed the cousin, expecting to hear anything from his cousin except that. "The marines? With the war going on, and so many people killed all over the place, you want to go in the marines. Are you crazy or something?"

"I made up my mind. I ain't gettin' any place here. Besides, I'm having a hard time at home. I can't seem to get goin'."

"Get goin'?" Michael repeated. "How old are you?"

Not even seventeen and you wanna 'get goin'? I like you wantin' to *get going,* but not the marines, not to be shot at."

"Come on, uncle Mike. The marines will be good for me."

At those words, his three small cousins cheered, causing the mother to intervene.

"Figlio mio... My son, we lost so many friends and relatives during the First World War. We don't want to lose you. Let the others fight. You stay home with us. Look at you, you're so handsome and strong, with that nice black long hair. Stay home. We'll find you a nice gal," she said.

Those words brought a smile to Rocky's face.

"You have a gal, eh?" she asked, winking.

"I don't."

"Yes you do, that Jugus gal. I know."

Rocky smiled and said nothing. Then he turned to his cousin and asked him about the fight with Billy Hays scheduled that evening. Reassuring Rocky he would be there, Michael tried to dissuade his cousin from joining the marines, to no avail.

After breakfast, Rocky went to Wilkes Barre, North Main Street. On approaching the Veterans Building, Rocky saw a lot of young men mingling by the front entrance. Gathering courage, he walked in to learn that to enlist one had to be seventeen years old. Undaunted, he went back to talk with his cousin Michael, who suggested to go see Father Dolan at St. Anna's.

Father Dolan gave Rocky a very warm welcome, wrapping his arms around the young man's large shoulders. "What can I do for you?" he asked.

"I wanna join the marines but I'm not seventeen and they won't take me," he said with one eye toward his uncle Michael.

"So," Father Dolan commented.

"I need a document with a new birth date, like a new Birth certificate."

"Yes Rocky, but I can't change the date!"

"Just write me out a new one; I'll change the date."

"What do you mean?" asked Father Dolan, who knew exactly what Rocky was talking about. He had already done Baptismal ones but not Birth certificates, and wanted to be sure the young man did not have another scheme.

"When you write the *seven* just write it lightly. I will write a *six* over it, and no one will know the difference," Rocky explained, causing his cousin and Father Dolan to laugh.

"As one would say in Italian, *Va bene?*"

"*Si, va bene...* It's all right. Then you'll do it?"

"No, Attilio, I will not. It is against the law. But, what I can do is give you a new Baptismal paper, okay?"

"What's the difference?" Rocky asked.

The priest proceeded to get out a new document, filling it out patiently and meticulously, being sure to leave the last digit barely legible. Then looking at Michael, Father Dolan commented that if the Italian kid from the coal fields wanted to join the Marines and fight for his country, a little early in life, and not wait until he was officially 17, he didn't mind, being sure that the U. S. Government couldn't have minded either.

Late that afternoon, after altering the certificate, he and his cousin returned to the Veterans Building where they got the necessary forms for the induction. Because, the kid needed his father's permission, the recruiting sergeant pulled ou. the form and told the kid exactly where Mr. Castellani had to sign.

At home, after asking his sisters to go to their room, Rocky apologized to his father for what happened with Marianna. Mr. Castellani told him that she had dropped all charges and that everything was fine. When Rocky— with his cousin seeming anxious— told Mr. Castellani that he had decided to join the Service, Mr. Castellani was shocked.

77

"*Vuoi fare il soldato*... You want to be a soldier. Are you crazy? You're the only son— my other two died— and you want to go to war... to die? Attilio, please! Attilio, we lost your mother; we don't want to lose you. Don't go!"

"I made up my mind. I really want to go. See these papers? The priest allowed me to fix my certificate, and all you have to do is sign here... here! After that, I'll be a marine."

"*Attilio, sei troppo giovane... You're too young to go in the Army...*"

"*The Marines* Pop! The marines! I want to join the marines. I beg you, please sign the papers."

Mr. Castellani looked deep into the eyes of his son; then he turned to his nephew, who nodded. At that moment, Mr. Castellani started to cry, tears rolling down his face. Seeing his boy standing there— the boy that was alive by a miracle, the boy whom Rose and he had loved so much and suffered so much knowing she would have had to leave him— now, that boy wanted to go off to war. *"Ma perchè*... But why?" he asked, knowing there was no answer other than to sign. *"Firmo*... I'll sign," he finally said, sobbing.

Rocky, feeling sadder than ever, quickly placed the form on the kitchen table, pulled out the pen the recruiting sergeant had given him, and gave it to the reluctant Mr. Castellani, who signed. A tear fell on the form, smudging part of it. With that done, Mr. Castellani brought his arms around Rocky. Holding him close, he sobbed. Moved by that embrace, Michael joined in and put his arms around the father and the son, telling them that everything was going to be alright, not to worry. In Mr. Castellani's heart, however, there was no joy; yet, he was able to contain his desperation. He had been through so much; now this.

Rocky broke his father's hold and went to see his sisters. Michael attempted to reassure Attilio that he had done the right thing. Unable to answer with words, Mr. Castellani simply put his arms around his nephew and held him. He broke away when his children came in. On seeing the father in tears, Yolanda quickly asked what happened.

"I'm going to be a marine," answered Rocky.

"You're going in the marines?" asked Anna.

"Yes, in the marines— a marine! Papa signed the papers. I'll be off in a few weeks. You two have to take good care of him. Promise?" asked Rocky.

Yolanda first and then Anna promised they would. Though they had a sober expression on their faces, inside they felt a certain excitement knowing their brother was going off to the Service, that he'd be a soldier, that he'd be wearing a uniform. They moved to Rocky's sides and each held his hands, the three standing in front of their father, who had stopped crying.

"Papa, tutto andrà bene... Everything will be fine," Yolanda said. *"Non preoccuparti...* Don't worry," she assured, a slight smile on her face. When she saw her father nodding, she put her arms around him.

A few minutes later, when Mr. Castellani was alone with his nephew, he began to talk. Reflectively sad, he commented much as he had done other times under stress, *"Questa è l'America...* This is America."

Michael, who had entered the mainstream and was therefore "Americanized", understood very well how his brother felt, even though he himself was still struggling. Life was not easy. *"La vita non è facile...* Life is not easy, Attilio. We have to do the best we can. With your son in the marines you can be sure they will take care of him— better than we can. Just think, you'll have one less mouth to feed, which means you'll be able to do a better job with the two girls."

"Lo so, lo so... I know, I know. I know he'll be better off in the Army. He'll be the better for it, unless he gets killed. But he'll come back, I know it," he said. Then turning introspective, and while looking deeply into the eyes of Michael he repeated to himself,

That evening, Rocky and Michael appeared at the gym. When the announcer gave the names of Billy Hayes from Scranton and of Roxy Wargo from Luzerne, the crowd cheered. Michael, in the corner, whispered into Rocky's ear, "This is one of your last fights before you're off. Make it a good one."

"I will," Rocky answered, sure of himself.

"Don't let *Roxy Wargo* down!" Michael said jokingly, causing him to smile, knowing that this might be his young cousin's last fight under that name.

The fight went four hard-fought rounds. Billy Hayes was very strong. His punches to Rocky's body were solid and effective. In the fourth round, however, Rocky connected on the chin with a deadly punch, causing Billy to drop to the canvass for a short count. When he resumed fighting, however, he seemed disoriented. The referee moved in and called the fight, to the joy of Rocky, his cousin Michael and the many fans.

When he got home, he found his father and sisters alone. Seeing that Marianna was not there, he felt relieved. Yolanda, of course, quickly ran to him and put her arms joyfully around her brother. Apparently, he had won.

Before leaving for the marines, on April 17, 1944, he fought George Henry to a draw.

The day prior to his induction, Rocky spent his time visiting his friends in their homes. Wherever he went, he almost always got the same story: the mothers of his friends told him not to go; his buddies and the younger kids all told him he had made the right decision. At Phil Paratore's house, Mrs. Paratore prepared a quick dinner, thus forcing Rocky to remain longer than he had planned. "You stay here and eat; after, you can go see your other friends," she said.

Having no alternative than to stay, Rocky nodded with a smile. Phil, who was standing next to him, put his arm around Rocky's shoulder and led him to the couch, telling his buddy that he too had thought of joining the marines, but simply didn't dare go any further, because he wasn't 17 yet.

"Who did you see so far?" Phil asked.

"Everyone— Goomby, Goombian, Red, etc. I guess I've seen them all," Rocky said, not sure of himself.

"No one else to see? Good, then you can spend the rest of the day with us," Phil suggested.

"No, I don't think I can. I think I'd like to go by Mary Jugus and say goodby."

"Mary Jugus?" Phil questioned, a slight frown on his forehead.

"Ya, Mary. Remember, her father was killed in the mines."

His stomach full, Rocky thanked Mrs. Paratore for the delicious meal. He hugged her and said goodby. At the door, he hugged Phil. Promising each other to keep in touch, Rocky left to go see Mary.

On the way over, he wasn't sure just what to say. He didn't even know if she was going to be home. When he reached the house, he was hesitant to knock on the door. Circumspect, he finally knocked. In a few seconds, Mrs. Jugus opened the door.

"May I help you?" she asked, not recognizing Rocky.

"Hi, my name is Attilio Castellani. My father worked..."

"Sure, I know who you are. Come in," she said, effusing warmth and charm. "I hope nothing happened with your father. We know he's not feeling good. You know, if it's not accidents that kill them, that dreadful coal miners disease will get them sooner or later. Tell me, is he alright?"

"Yes, Mrs. Jugus. My father is well."

"Good," she said, curious about why he was there.

"Well," he began with a slight stutter. "I joined the marines and tomorrow I'll be leaving. I thought to say goodby to you... to all of you."

"Did you want to say goodby to Mary?" she asked with a smile.

Stuttering, he said he did. When Mrs. Jugus told him Mary was out, his face dropped.

"Don't be disappointed," she said. "You can come see her when you come back. Alright?"

Rocky nodded. Feeling awkward, he then stepped aside, turned around and left, saying a quiet goodbye.

Chapter 8

Basic Training

Having taken the train to Philadelphia, Rocky felt a certain excitement as he traveled away from home, among so many different and strange people. This was to be the beginning of a new adventure, and he felt good about it. On the train, he chatted with several other young men who had also joined the military and were on their way to different camps. On hearing Rocky say he was going to Parris Island, one of them called it a "Hell-hole". That remark startled Rocky, but more because he hadn't understood exactly the implication behind it. Nor was he particularly disturbed when the same young man commented on Rocky's long hair.

After about a day's ride, Rocky finally reached South Carolina where he then took a bus to Parris Island. He looked out the window, noticing how different the landscape was from that of his hometown.

Upon arrival, a typical tough-looking First Sergeant ordered the new recruits to form a line.

"When I give the command, *attention*," he said in a rough voice, "it means you are to stand straight up and not move one muscle in your bodies."

The sergeant moved from the left to the right, stopping in front of each new marine, telling each exactly what to do and where to do it. When he reached Rocky, he told him to get a haircut, telling him where the barber was. When he finished, he ordered them to march to the barracks. After ordering *at ease,* he gave them further instruction on their bedding, the mess hall, etc. "By 1700 hours, you will all be back here, looking clean and with your haircuts."

After dismissal, Rocky scrambled into the barrack looking for his bed. Instead, he found his bunk with a mattress rolled up on the spring, a steel locker with the door open, and an empty box on the floor.

"Heck," complained one, "the bed is not made," causing a few to begin to laugh, including Rocky.

After unrolling the mattress, he first placed the sheets and then the blanket, leaving the pillow on top of the blanket. Satisfied with how it looked, he left to go to the barber. On passing by the office, he was stopped by a corporal in charge of quarters. "I'm the CQ," he said. "Where are you going?"

"To the barber shop," Rocky said.

"Barber shop?" the CQ repeated. "You're not home. There are no barber shops here. The barber is two barracks down on your left."

On entering the mirrorless *shop,* he noticed a marine gathering a lot of long hair with his wide broom which he pushed in short jerky movements around a whole bunch of men sitting rigidly on chairs with the barbers in T-shirts cutting across their heads with electric razors. When it came to his turn, Rocky hesitated.

"Next!" called the barber, rudely.

Rushing to his barracks with his hand over his semi bald head, Rocky ran into the latrine to look in the mirror. As he looked, he could hardly recognize himself. What stood out, however— but he was not aware of it— were his big deep brown eyes.

On the way to his bunk, his future buddies began to laugh. Rocky smiled.

Still in civilian clothes, the new marines lined up

outside the mess hall, admitted one at a time by the mess sergeant who had each marine sign the voucher. Rocky simply watched what others did and followed suit. With a stainless steel tray in his hand, he saw the amount of food in front of him, and proceeded to take whatever was dished out: meat, potatoes, greens, bread, pudding, milk, etc. He had never seen so much food as now. At the table, he ate everything, including the extra bread and potatoes from a buddy next to him.

The following day, Rocky and his buddies followed a tight schedule of drawing their gear, going to classes, getting instruction on how to maintain their quarters, and getting their assignments, including KP (kitchen police). By evening, Rocky felt he had nothing to worry about, nothing to think about, not even home because he knew he wouldn't have any time to stand still and think.

Cocky Young Kid

Called *Jarhead* by non-marines, Rocky was not bothered by that reference. He liked what he had gotten into; in fact, he loved it. He was made and built just for that kind of military duty.

Because of his quiet ways, the other marines soon began to like him. As they went through their rigorous training, be it on post or in the field, Rocky was always unassuming, doing his job and hardly ever talking or challenging anyone. The thing that really impressed his buddies, however, was the speed and preciseness with which he accomplished the various field exercises on the ranges and on the many marches. Young Rocky was in such tremendous shape that he almost always finished at the top. His buddies, however, really began to pay attention to him when— after about the first rigorous month of unending combat training— learned he had been boxing in Pennslavania.

Though his time was completely taken with that

training, Rocky always found time to think about his family. One night, at about three in the morning, lying awake on his bunk looking at the ceiling, he thought of his mother, his father and sisters, remembering the scene when he asked his father to sign the forms, and how he cried. He couldn't understand why his father had cried so much. Now that he had spent enough time training, with the heavy emphasis on *Kill! Kill!,* he was beginning to understand his father's concerns: he feared his son would never be back. "Kill or be killed" stood in his mind together with the memories of his folks. Suddenly the bugle sounded, startling Rocky. It was four in the morning and a new day of training and indoctrination was just beginning.

May 28, 1944, Rocky's birthday, went unobserved. On that day, however, the drill sergeant began pairing off for hand to hand combat, first directed by the drill sergeant, then all of the marines thrown together in a melee, the only goal was to subdue as many opponents as possible. Weighing only 126 pounds, just the minimum weight to meet United States Marine Corps (USMC) standards, Rocky won big. His agility, balance and power impressed everyone, including the Non- Commissioned Officers and Officers supervising the training.

With the bootcamp about over, there was a lot of talk concerning assignments. Word got out that most of them were going to be shipped to the Pacific to fight the *Japs.* When Rocky understood the situation—meaning, to go against Europe or Japan, he was relieved. Being of Italian background, he certainly would not have wanted to go fight in Europe. What he didn't know, however, was that the Government made all kinds of efforts to send Americans of Italian or of German descent to the Pacific, and many of Oriental descent to Europe.

When the trainees also learned that at the end of bootcamp they would possibly have a 10 day leave, many opted for various places: visiting their homes.

Rocky was somewhat slow in understanding *leave*. When he finally did, suddenly he felt confused. He wanted to go see his family. He imagined how it would be to go home in uniform, how happy they would be to see him. In any event, there was still time left and a lot more training before that time.

After having completed firing the M-1 rifle and winning the Expert Badge, Rocky and his buddies were ordered to get ready for night maneuvers which included search and destroy and a run on the ground with live machine gun fire overhead. The latter became of great concern with everyone. They asked what if there were short rounds, or if someone would mistakenly point the machine guns downward. What would happen?

"We'd be killed," answered Rocky matter-of-factly, but with a grin on his face. "Look," he said, in an attempt to relieve them from that fear, "our time will come, and I don't think it's gonna be here."

At the end of a five mile night hike with full field-pack weighing about 50 pounds, the drill sergeant ordered the men to rest for 15 minutes. When the time was up, he gathered his troops and went over procedures and techniques on how to complete— without casualties— the *live* phase of the next exercise.

"Remember," he said in a rough voice, "you'll be crawling under barbed wire. There'll be close and continuous live machine gun fire overhead. If you get your head up, or your arm, or get your but up a little too much, you run the risk of being hit. Do you all understand? You have to crawl, sticking to the ground. Keep your faces down and move foreword as rapidly as possible. Is that clear?"

With projectiles whistling overhead, the trainees began their crawl, their hearts in their mouths. Making sure to know who his buddies next to him were, Rocky began his crawl, his long arms easily pulling him ahead, his face close to the soil, his neck sweating. At a point, his backpack got stuck on the barbed wire.

With the help of his buddy who extended his arm to push the pack down, Rocky continued the crawl without a hitch. On arriving at the end, young Rocky Castellani waited for his buddy to thank him for the help.

By 11 PM, the unit moved to a camp site where teams of two men pitched their tents. By one o'clock, the exhausted marines finally got to sleep. At four, the bugle sounded to begin another day.

Hungry and tired, they continued their training until five thirty when the sergeant ordered a break for chow. While many complained about the K-rations, Rocky simply devoured all he had as well as those given him by his buddies.

During those weeks of continuous training, Rocky put on a few more pounds. He felt so good, that he easily out-distanced everyone in his platoon in the exercises requiring physical stamina and strength.

For the first time in his life, he felt a real excitement about living. Not knowing where he would go upon graduation made life more fascinating.

When all the results were in, Rocky scored in the top ten percent of his training battalion— not bad for a kid who had been brought up in a poor family that didn't speak English, who hadn't even finished high school. The fact that he applied himself surely must have made the difference.

Graduation day was set for Saturday afternoon. In their sharp Class-A uniforms, spit-shined boots, they stood tall in front of the reviewing stand filled with the top brass of the command and many parents and relatives. Standing in the middle of his formation— he was only about five feet eight inches tall— he stood at attention, proud to listen to the high ranking officers bestowing their praises on a job well done. He felt even inspired when the commanding officer spoke about the fight in Europe and in the Pacific and how the United States had to fight to preserve liberty for itself and the rest of the world.

"Many of you will be going to the Pacific," the punctilious Commanding Officer said. "The fact that you completed the training at Parris Island is proof that you will be able to take just about anything the enemy will offer, be they German or Japanese. I am sure, you will bring honor on yourselves, your families, the Marine Corps and this great country of ours— the United States of America."

After the various awards were presented, the Commanding Officer ordered the troops to pass in review. The band leader blew the whistle and the drummer quickly executed with a heavy beat of the drums. With the wind instruments clamoring in concert, the various commanders began to shout their orders. Leading off with their left, the men of the first unit moved forward. At a given moment, the commander ordered a right turn down the field until he ordered a first left turn. With the second left turn, the unit marched forward toward the reviewing stand. In the middle of what seemed like thousands of marines, Rocky felt as though he was one in spirit and motion with the rest. Although he could not see the reviewing stand from where he was marching, when he heard the command "Eyes Right", he turned his head. With his chest expanded to its limit, he stepped forward with pride and confidence.

After the parade, they returned to their respective barracks to learn about their assignments— Europe or the Pacific. Rocky and a few of his buddies lingered outside the front door, chatting about their plans.

"I hope it'll be the Pacific," Rocky commented.

"Yeah," the other marine answered. "With the *duce* in Italy, it's better you go fight the Japs. We wouldn't want you to get cold feet... In any event, Rocky, where are you going on your leave?"

"I'm goin' home," he answered without hesitation. "I'm sure I won't be going to Europe, so I'll get to see California. How about you guys: who's going home?"

At that moment, the sergeant called from the inside.

The orders were ready. On hearing he got the Pacific, Rocky smiled.

"Are you happy?" the sergeant asked in a kind voice. Not expecting that tone, Rocky looked up in disbelief. He paused a second, then nodded with a smile. The sergeant padded Rocky on the back affectionately, pushing him out the door. "I feel you're going to bring credit to the Marine Corps," he said. "I wish you luck, Rocky. You will make a good marine."

Happy over those words, Rocky went to his bunk. While getting his things ready for the move the next morning, he thought about his mother and father, how happy they would have been if they could have seen him on the parade ground that afternoon. "Well, at least my father will see me in uniform when I get home," he said to himself, trying to envision how his father and two sisters would react to seeing him.

Early the next morning, after they cleared quarters and brought the duffel bags to be processed out, dressed in their Class-A uniforms, they all divided into groups and headed for the buses. When Rocky's bus passed the front gate of Parris Island, the marines gave a shout of boisterous joy, except for Rocky, who simply sat quietly as the bus passed through the gate.

After several hours on the train, Rocky reached Wilkes Barre about noon. He got off the train and walked around the square, his steps measured and deliberate. He got the connecting bus into Kingston and then to Luzerne, a short trip.

Most of his young life, he had to jump on a coal truck to hitch a ride. Now, he had money to travel first class, which is exactly how he felt when he got off the bus. In no time, he met with a few of his old chums who asked all kinds of questions about Parris Island and the training. They looked him over, impressed by the uniform and by the way he looked. Feeling admired, he expanded his chest a little, agreeing to meet with them that evening.

On arriving home, he walked up the steps, opened the door and walked in. Standing in the doorway, he called out if anyone was home. In a few seconds, Yolanda appeared from the bedroom. On seeing her brother in uniform, she felt overwhelmed with joy. With a great big smile on her face, she rushed toward him. He extended his arms, wrapped them around her waist and lifted her in the air in a semicircle.

"Attilio!" she exclaimed, "I'm so happy to see you. You're so beautiful!"

After he put her down, he asked where everyone was.

"You don't know," she said in a sad tone, "Anna left. She couldn't take school no more, and got married. Papa is at the doctor. You know, he got that stuff called *sillacosus.*"

"Silicosis! You know, the disease of the lungs, from working in the coal mines."

After a few minutes of affectionate conversation, noticing he was tired, Yolanda told him to take a nap. Rocky took off his uniform, and lay on his bed. With his face turned upward, he thought of the irony of the whole thing. There he was, having just returned from boot camp, wearing his sharp marine uniform, wanting to make an impression on his father, and he wasn't even home— he was at the doctor supposedly with an illness that too often was fatal. As he stared at the ceiling, he also thought of his mother, wishing she had been there to receive him, to show her that he had been successful and that he was a good son. With his eyes closed he tried to understand what was happening to his family, knowing that two of his sisters had married prematurely. "Oh, if only our mother were here!" he said to himself. He opened his eyes knowing he could do nothing against an unkind, if not blind, fate. As young as he was, he understood all of these things, and more. He understood that he had no choice but to continue with his life, thanking God for all the things which were happening to him. He thanked God for his health, knowing that with his strong body one day he would be able to put it to good use— hopefully, even to make his father proud of him.

"Well," he thought as he closed his eyes, "he will see me in uniform when I leave."

After about two hours, a few of his buddies began to arrive. Yolanda tip toed to Rocky's bed, stopping to look at her famous brother, admiring his good looks even though she did not particularly like his semi bald head. She then turned to look at the uniform he had placed on a hanger on the closet door, her eyes stopping on the shiny brass. "Attilio," she said gently as she placed her hand softly on his face. "Attilio, your friends are here," she said softly, her eyes glowing with quiet admiration. "Attilio!" she repeated, placing her hand over her brother's forehead.

With a slight jump, Rocky awoke. "My God!" he remarked, still dazed from his heavy sleep. "What time is it?"

After telling him about his friends, Yolanda started to leave the room.

"Where's pop?" he asked. "Isn't he back yet?"

"No, but he probably won't be back till late. You just go out and have a good time. Do you want to eat something first?"

"And you, what will you be doing?" asked Rocky.

"Nothing, I just stay home."

"And what do you do?"

"I study. I like books," his kid sister answered.

"What do you know," he commented with a great big smile. "We have a student in the family. I'd love to see you get your high school diploma," he said, knowing that she would.

With that, Yolanda left her brother to wash up and to get dressed. When he appeared, his friends went to shake his hand, congratulating him for having finished boot camp. He looked at them all, grinning over their long hair, causing them to laugh.

With Phil, Goombian, and the rest, the group left for downtown, stopping at the local cafeteria. When Rocky came up to the register to pay, his friends stopped him.

"It's on us," Phil yelled with a big grin.

After they ate, they talked about going to the movies or something, finally settling on going to the local gym where Rocky had spent so much time. When they got there, Rocky was happily surprised to see Father Dolan, who proudly put his arms around the young marine.

When Rocky got home at about one o'clock, he peeked into the bedroom. Seeing Yolanda sleeping, he then peeked into his father's room. Seeing he had not yet returned, Rocky went to his bed, disappointed.

Soon after, Mr. Castellani returned. Sensing something different in the house, he went to check on Yolanda. Satisfied she was sleeping, he turned to Rocky's room. He walked to the bed. When he saw his son sound asleep, he became emotional. His son had come home, and he hadn't been there. He wanted to touch him. He extended his hand hesitantly. As he was about to place it on Rocky's forehead, he stopped. Tears began to fall down his face. He withdrew his hand, and went back to his room, without making a noise.

At about six o'clock in the morning, Rocky woke up. When he realized he was no longer at boot camp, he turned to one side and fell asleep again.

Yolanda, who had gotten up a little earlier, after seeing her brother still sleeping, went to the corner store to get fresh Italian bread and eggs.

Having prepared breakfast— fried eggs with home fries, she first went to Rocky and then to her father, then returned to the kitchen to wait.

On seeing his father, Rocky extended his arms. Mr. Castellani hugged his big son and held him close to his chest, telling him, in Italian, how happy he was to see him.

"I'm so happy to see you too, Pop," Rocky said, pushing his father back so he could look at him. "You went to the doctor last night," he said. "How are you?"

"*Sto bene*... I am well. You know about the mines. But don't worry. I'll be fine. The doctor said I'll be around for a long time," he said with a proud smile. "You look so strong!"

As soon as they sat at the table, Yolanda served them breakfast. Rocky got a large slice of Italian bread, dipped its heavy crust into the soft yellow of the egg and began to eat, his father pouring two glasses of wine.

"*Allora*... Then," Mr. Castellani said, "after you put on your uniform, we'll go visit your uncle Michael Castellani and see a few friends, and your cousin Michael Costello."

Between one visit and another, with a lot of time spent with his friends who were still in high school, Rocky found himself with one day left. Proudly wearing his uniform, he went to visit Mary Yugus.

Unsure of himself, he knocked on the door. In a few seconds, Mrs. Yugus opened the door. On seeing Rocky in uniform, she jerked her head back a little from the surprise.

"Well," she commented, a great smile on her face. "You're Attilio Castellani. You came to see Mary before you left for the service."

"Yes Mrs. Jugus. I'm the same one. Is Mary home? I would like to see her."

"I'm sorry son, but she's not home. She works and she won't be home until late this evening. You can come tomorrow afternoon if you wish. I'll tell her you were here."

"No, I guess I won't be seeing her this time. I'm leaving tomorrow morning."

"How long have you been here?" she asked abruptly.

"A few days," he answered embarrassed, knowing he had goofed, his forehead full of wrinkles.

Sensing Rocky's embarrassment, Mrs. Jugus quickly took him by the hand and lead him into the house. "Come in," she said. "I'll fix you something to eat."

"Many thanks, Mrs. Jugus, but I'm meeting with my friends. We're going out to eat. Tell Mary I was in to see her," he said in a low voice. He turned around and walked out the door.

"I'll tell her you were here," Mrs. Jugus said. She stood there puzzled, looking at young Rocky leaving her house. Although he was young, he looked like a man, and somehow felt that Rocky, for some unknown reason— was going to enter their lives. The thought of it happening pleased her, as she watched Rocky Castellani walking tall down the street.

Early morning, uncle Mike stopped at the house to see Rocky. With Mr. Castellani sadly proud, the three men sat around the kitchen table while Yolanda, full of smiles, went on preparing breakfast— eggs with home fries, Italian bread and wine. Michael, however, asked for espresso coffee.

"*Mio figlio*... My son," said Mr. Castellani as he looked at him. "He looks good in the marine uniform, doesn't he?"

"He does. He's a good boy," Michael commented. "We're all proud of him... Tell me Attilio, how was the food at boot camp?"

"It was good," the kid answered with enthusiasm. When he realized that by so saying he was knocking the food he had had at home, he began to qualify his statement. In his heart he knew, however, that he had never eaten as much and as well at home as he did in the marines. "You know, uncle Michael, a lot of guys don't like the chow in the marines."

"Chow! What's that?" asked Mr. Castellani.

"That's Army food," interrupted Yolanda, causing the three to laugh.

The time came for Rocky to leave. Mr. Castellani

gave his son a prolonged hug, telling him to be careful and to come back in one piece. When Mr. Castellani released him, Rocky turned to Yolanda to hug her. Together with his cousin Mike, Rocky went out the door. Yolanda and Mr. Castellani stood on the porch watching the two men walk away. While Yolanda succeeded in holding back her tears— though she felt a lump in her throat, Mr. Castellani began to cry. Yolanda looked up.

"Come pop, let's go in."

Chapter 9

The Pacific Campaign

When Rocky arrived at the New River Camp, North Carolina, he showed the guards his papers and was quickly told to report to Building A for duty. For the next couple of days, together with thousands of other marines, Rocky cleaned the yards and did a lot of menial jobs while he waited for orders to ship out. Orders quickly came. As it happened, the day was cloudy and windy. Heavy rain came and went. For four hours, the marines loaded the assigned materiel on a train for the long haul across the United States to California. In spite of the elements, Rocky accomplished his duties without ever complaining, even when he had to stand in the chow line under the rain for a prolonged period of time.

After about four days on the train, wherein Rocky passed the time telling stories, playing cards and wondering how it would be to fight the Japanese, the marines arrived at Camp Pendleton in San Diego.

Soon after, Rocky found himself on board the *Blue Fountain* docked at the San Diego Harbor together with three other similar ships. Full of sweat, as it was unusually hot that day, Rocky looked at the ship, awed by its size and by the large number of marines it was carrying.

Squeezed like sardines, Rocky shared one of the six high bunks down deep in the ship where ventilation wasn't a word. Early the next morning, in a dense fog, three big tug boats pushed *The Blue Fountain* toward the open Pacific, on the way to Hawaii, then to the Mariana Islands, with the Island of Guam as the final destination.

Outside of the usual menial work every marine had to accomplish while on board, the officers scheduled several kinds of activities to keep the marines busy. One of these was boxing. Taken by the events of moving out, he had practically forgotten about his great love. When one of the non-commissioned officers announced the boxing matches, young Rocky naturally volunteered to participate. Having won the first few bouts, Rocky began to be the center of conversations among the marines. On one occasion, this rather tough looking marine engaged a few others in idle conversation. Bragging about his sports feats, he asked Rocky to tell his buddies about his boxing. When Rocky simply answered that he liked to fight and that he had been doing it while in school, the marine challenged Rocky to be more specific about boxing, wanting exact details.

"Look, I don't know what you're talking about," Rocky answered, annoyed by the insistent and arrogant tone of his fellow marine.

"I bet you're the same about girls," mused the marine with a derisive laugh, causing the others to laugh likewise.

Defensive, but not wanting to partake of that kind of conversation, Rocky shrugged his shoulder without answering.

"You're Italian, aren't you?" the marine asked.

"Ya, what of it!" Rocky answered in a firm tone.

"Well, all I heard was that *whaps* are great lovers."

"And they're also good fighters," Rocky retorted. Then in an instant, he let his right fist go directly and with deadly accuracy to the chin of the braggart.

With his fists ready, Rocky waited for him to stand up. Instead, he launched at Rocky grabbing him around the waist with his strong arms, wrestling Rocky to the deck, causing a certain commotion among the rest. A few officers intervened, breaking up the fight.

Word was out about Rocky's boxing ability and style. Unbeknown to him, the officer in charge of the sports program, Lieutenant Angelo Bartelli, All American, and the first winner of the coveted Heisman Trophy, was also in charge of discipline.

"Water and bread," ordered Bartelli, his voice full blast at Rocky, who was standing at attention.

"Oh no!" Rocky cried out. "I've lived on bread and water most of my life. I ain't gonna do that now. Besides, I was only 16 when I enlisted; I lied about age. I didn't do anything wrong, Sir; I'd go home first. He started it. It's not my fault."

When the other marine apologized to Rocky, Bartelli decided to drop the charges, but with a sharp warning against similar recurrences.

Having been aware of Rocky's boxing, Bartelli made it a point to closely watch the next bout. Mixing himself with the rest of the troops, he watched Rocky handle a bigger and more powerful marine. He particularly liked seeing young Rocky show restraint: the smaller Italian kid could have knocked down his opponent but didn't. Impressed, Bartelli quickly had young Rocky reassigned.

Rocky, who had been trained as a infantryman, was scheduled to be on the first assault of the up-coming battle. Bartelli had him reassigned 100 yeards behind the front line. As a result, he did not take part of the first wave. Neither did he know about Bartelli's secret hopes to have him assigned to his company.

Battle of Guam

Young Rocky was part of the Third Marine Division. On July 21, 1944, as part of the Southern

Troops, the Division, with its three regiments abreast, was scheduled to land on the western beaches of the Island of Guam.

By mid July 1944, the American campaign to seize the Marianas was one third completed. Saipan had fallen and the invasion of neighboring Tinian was imminent. In the meantime, plans called for the recapture of Guam, which had been held by the Japanese since December 10, 1941. Because of its strategic location in relation to Japan, Guam, which by now was heavily fortified, became a focal point of the Pacific campaign. With its capture, it would give the U.S. Forces both naval and air superiority. The mission was assigned to Major General Roy S. Geiger of the Third Amphibious Corps which comprised the Third Marine Division under Major General Allen H. Turnage, and the First Provisional Marine Brigade under Brigadier General L. C. Shepherd, Jr. The task of landing and protecting the troops was given to Brigadier General Pedro A. Del Valle, commander of the Third Amphibious Corps Artillery, to Major General Andrew D. Bruce, commander of the 77th Infantry Division, and to Rear Admiral Richard L. Connolly, commander of the Naval Task Force.

The Japanese force, about 18,000 strong, was commanded by Lieutenant General Takeshi Takashina, who had withstood about two weeks of some of the U.S. Navy's heaviest bombardment which considerably weakened the Japanese defense. All of the big Japanese guns were either destroyed or damaged.

The night before the landing, Rocky lay on his bunk, his eyes staring at the bottom of the bunk above, thinking about the landing. The words of "Kill, Kill" from his boot camp days flashed through his mind. Now he was going to participate in his first battle, knowing he was going to see a lot of death. He thought of his mother and knew that this was different. In his young mind, he was able to rationalize between the two kinds of death— his mother's, which was not

A Marine Sherman tank blasts a Japanese pillbox in advance of 3d Division infrantrymen on Guam in August 1944. Marine at right carries a souvenir Japanese sword on his pack.

wanted by anyone including his mother herself, and the pending battle, which was created through a series of conscious decisions. Just as his mother was helpless in her fight against her fatal illness, he was helpless against the impending battle with its consequent death. "Oh well," he said to himself, not knowing that in much of his behavior and character, he resembled her very much.

The Division was scheduled to land at dawn. The marines were loaded into their *Higgins Boats* for the assault. At 08:30, the first wave of the invasion began moving toward their assigned sectors on the beaches under powerful barrages of protective fire power. The Third Division landed on the west coast between Adelpus Point and Asan Point, with the First Marine Brigade landing further south between Point Bangi and the town of Agana. At both points, the Japanese first answered with sporadic shelling, hitting several of the landing crafts. As more marines came ashore, the Japanese intensified their fire power. By night fall, however, the U.S. marines had secured their objectives and quickly prepared for the enemy's counterattack. It came as expected. However, although the Japanese were successful in hitting one sector, the main thrust of their attack was repulsed.

In the following several days, the marines slowly gained more and more territory, losing more and more men in the process, but inflicting major casualties on the enemy.

With the 77th Division completely ashore, its main mission was to gain control of all southern Guam. Unexpectedly, the Japanese launched a heavy counter attack on the 3rd Division, breaking through several gaps. By morning, the big Japanese counter attack failed with a loss of more than 4,000 men.

On disembarking from *The Blue Fountain,* and engaging in battle, a Japanese artillery shell exploded in the vicinity of Rocky's position, killing and wounding several of his buddies. On seeing some blown to bits, Rocky shuddered. Just as he asked himself if he were next, the platoon sergeant yelled an order to continue the fire. Immediately, Rocky obeyed, continuing as though neither the enemy's blistering and deafening firepower nor that of his own making existed. When attacks finally stopped, Rocky and his buddies stared at each other incredulously. They could not believe they were alive.

"Are you all OK?" called the sergeant.

Rocky just looked at the sergeant, who then asked the same question of the others who answered in the affirmative.

With the 77th pushing north, the marines consolidated their lines and began the mopping up of small pockets of resistance. When the First Brigade reached Ritidian Point in the northernmost point of the island, the Battle of Guam was over.

In this ferocious battle, America had 1,400 soldiers killed and more than 6,500 wounded. Among the dead and the wounded were several of Rocky's buddies.

"How could I ever forget them?" he said to himself, while resting in his tenth, K-rations cans and cartons to one side, his rifle next to his right. "I got through this one. What's next?"

Around the middle of August, with Guam completely secured, the commanding officers began a new phase of training, apparently to get ready for the next battle.

Seventeen years old, and with the battle of Guam under his belt, young Rocky volunteered to participate in the boxing matches scheduled as part of the training program. He didn't know, however, that Lt. Bartelli had requested and received permission to have Rocky fight for his outfit.

Although Bartelli's aim, for the 30 or more bouts he had scheduled, was simply to keep them in good physical shape and to have fun at the same time, he was delighted to see his Italian *paesano* participate in them without any difficulty.

"It must be all the rations Rocky's eating," commented Bartelli one afternoon, seeing that Rocky was also eating portions of what other soldiers were giving him. "It seems you're always hungry," Bartelli commented.

"Not that I was hungry the past sixteen years, but let's say I didn't really have that much food. So, if it's available, I'll eat."

"Whatever it is, these rations must be doing you a lot of good," Bartelli commented as he looked at Rocky's body. "You look mighty fit."

Rocky was well liked. He was easy going, quite, trustworthy and unassuming. For a seventeen-year-old, he was very mature physically and intellectually. Above all, he had a good philosophy about life in that he did the things he could do and did them well. For these reasons, he was liked both by his peers and his superiors. Lt. Bartelli, of course, liked him even more because Rocky was of Italian descent, although he would not say it aloud to his colleagues.

For several weeks, Rocky completed the scheduled training. Although he thrived on boxing, he also enjoyed jogging along the beaches and visiting the various locales. He was impressed to learn that Magellan had discovered Guam in 1521, that the people were predominantly Chamorro, descendants of the Micronesian stock mixed with Filipino, Spanish, American, Italian, British, Japanese, Chinese and Mexican. Perhaps above all, he enjoyed the climate, often making comparisons with the many cold nights he suffered in his native Pennsylvania.

Military life on Guam was not always that smooth. When things didn't go his way, he especially longed to be home with his family and friends; above all, to be back in school working for his diploma. His longing for home accentuated when he received his *Care* packages. The great outdoors, the sunshine, the service gymnasium, the food, even the quarters, however, made Rocky quickly forget about his hometown. "I don't even like the snow at Christmas time," he said to himself.

Christmas 1945 came around without much fanfare. The island was just too different from home. There was no snow, and it wasn't cold. For Rocky, besides, there was plenty of food and very good sports facilities. Because of his boxing feats, he was enjoying special privileges he had never dreamed he could have had.

On New Years Day, the Command made every effort in organizing appropriate festivities. It even made available cold beer for most of the troops. The older, more experienced troops, especially the corporals and the sergeants celebrated past midnight. Many formed groups and went from tent to tent to celebrate. Rocky, with a group of marines of his own age, did likewise except for one thing: he didn't drink. In their rompings from one tent to another, Rocky was almost always recognized by the other marines because of his boxing.

In fact, it was not just Bartelli, who sought out young Rocky. Several of the other Company Commanders requested that Rocky be assigned to their units. They had noticed that this young marine was both a superior fighting marine and a consummate boxer. What they seemed to like above all was Rocky's unassuming and quiet character. He would always complete his assignments without fanfare, exuding confidence in his buddies who made sure to talk about him and his accomplishments. In this respect, Rocky enjoyed a particular friendship with them, and commanded the attention of the officers as well. Rocky, however, neither knew nor understood he was being given special treatment, which made him that much more attractive and likable.

Rocky had become the hero of the welterweight division. For the next several months, boxing had become the central sport on Guam, with just about every serviceman participating. For Rocky, the program gave him the possibility to learn more about the sport and to acquire the skills necessary to become a champion. In this respect, Bartelli and several others who had had boxing experience were of immense help. Among the many lessons, Rocky learned to weigh the capabilities of his opponents and to gauge his timing so he didn't waste his energy during the first rounds, when a boxer's tendency is to go for the quick and early knock down.

In his early bouts, Rocky went into the first rounds with full fury, winning most of the fights and losing some by decisions. As he learned to pace himself, he became more effective, usually winning in the latter rounds by TKOs or unanimous decisions, thus pleasing the spectators and the top brass.

Life on Guam was not just fun and games. Whatever the marines did, they did it according to plans, and the plan was to keep them in tip top physical shape. The war was being fought throughout the world, and Guam was certainly not the last island to conquer. For that reason, training to achieve better weapons skills and physical stamina were emphasized. Rumors, as usual, floated around. But not one except the top brass knew of what was coming up.

"We aint' seen all of hell yet," yelled the platoon sergeant supervising mortar training.

"You mean more than what we saw during the Guam invasion?" Rocky commented to his partner.

"Who knows," he answered, as he handed the ammunition to Rocky, who was sweating around the neck.

The rumors persisted until February. Then all of a sudden: "Full Battle Gear". By four o'clock in the morning, the marines quietly broke camp. With the units formed and ready, the commanding officers began to march them out to an unknown destination. Still dark, the marines queried one another about what was happening, but each knowing as much as the next. When Rocky was asked the same question, he replied flatly that he didn't know and that soon enough they would all find out.

As the units of the Third Division marched across the island, they were joined by units of the Fourth and the Fifth Divisions. When Rocky saw what was happening, he, like the rest, quickly realized something big was in the making. They marched till dawn, stopping a short distance by a strange shore. There, they were ordered to bivouac, to chow down and not to make any noises— especially, not to smoke or make any light of any kind. Bunched in groups, Rocky and his buddies broke open their packs of rations. Somberly, they began to eat. When one asked Rocky if he wanted some of the crackers, they all began to smile. Looking up, Rocky extended his arm and laughed.

Under cover of darkness, the unit commanders whispered their orders to move out toward the beach. As the troops got close to the water, they could see the silhouttes of the Higgin's boats lined up for boarding. After wading to the boats, they were carried to the *Jefferson*. With full field gear and for the most part wet, the marines climbed the nets to get on board. When all the troops were accounted for and assignments made, the *Jefferson* steamed out into the open Pacific where it sailed for 14 days, with the marines not having the faintest idea where they were going.

Battle of Iwo Jima

After about ten days of sail, destination silence was finally lifted: Iwo Jima, a small island about 660 miles off the coast of Japan was to be their target.

According to military intelligence, the island's only value was its limited sulphur deposits. Its terrain was scarred by twisting gorges and broken ridges. In its southern tip loomed Mount Suribachi, an extinct volcano of about 550 feet. Since their take over, the Japanese had built two airfields, and had commenced a third. To defend the island, the Japanese constructed 642 blockhouses, pillboxes and other gun positions.

Iwo Jima, therefore, was not going to be taken by a marine assault alone. Combining air with naval, the Americans continued their continuous and merciless bombardments.

With each unit commander briefing their men on the up-coming battle, the troops felt unusually at ease, having resolved to do whatever their country asked them to do, whatever the cost.

"I'm tired of waitin' on this ship," commented Rocky. "I just wanna' get off and get the thing over with."

"We'll have our chances tomorrow," answered one.

Having some time to wander about, the marines mixed with those of other units as they had done throughout the voyage. While in the chow line, Rocky got a glimpse of a marine that looked like someone he knew. On approaching him, he discovered he was Gene Machinist from the same Wyoming Valley of Northeastern Pennsylvania, the two throwing their arms around each other with apparent happiness. Gene had also enlisted earlier and had been trained as a medic.

"If something happens to me, you'll take good care of me," Rocky jokingly asked.

"So long as you don't get your butt shot off," Gene answered with a wide grin across his face.

The two buddies were inseparable the rest of the night, spending most of their free time topside, recounting their stories about basic training. Their conversations, however, centered mainly about the people of their home town. Rocky asked about his father. Gene, of course, would not know anything about him. Rocky asked about some of the local crowd. Again, Gene had no information.

"Now look, I went into the service before you did, you know," Gene responded.

"Look," Rocky said, "the waves are pushing up. I guess we're in for a tough day tomorrow."

"I hope tomorrow won't be as bad as Guam," commented Gene, to Rocky's surprise. Gene had taken part in the recapture of the island, finding the whole situation ironic in that the island had belonged to the United States in the first place.

By early dawn, the waves had gotten higher. The Higgin's boats and smaller crafts tossed along side the *Jefferson,* while the men waited for the assault order. Suddenly, the Japanese opened fire. Artillery shells were exploding every where, several in front of the ship, right off the bow and to starboard. Rocky and Gene looked on, their hearts pounding. Fortunately, the ship was just outside enemy range, so most of the shells fell short.

With the waves causing havoc with the lighter crafts below, the commander hesitated in launching the assault. When the Japanese guns started to reach the ship, the men were ordered to take cover below. Rocky and Gene dashed toward the hatch together with the rest of the marines all pushing one another forward. A round suddenly exploded on the upper deck sending the marines diving for cover. One of the kids, between Gene and Rocky, got his left leg and side all shot up. Bleeding profusely, he screamed for help.

On seeing him losing blood, Gene quickly began to administer aid. But one of the officers quickly intervened, ordering the victim to be evacuated. Gene objected to no avail, for he too was ordered below.

With the *Jefferson* just outside reach of enemy fire, and though the waters were more agitated, the order was given to begin the assault.

Rocky and Gene made their way to the net and quickly rushed down to the tossing Higgin's boat below. When all the marines were on board, the boat began to move away from the ship and toward the shore. Unfortunately, because of the extremely choppy waters combined with a counter wind, the boat was not able to advance toward shore. After many tries and several hours of maneuvering, the Higgin's commander was ordered to get back. Wet, cold and demoralized, the marines began to climb up the net, their hands livid and hurting. When Rocky saw Gene having a hard time holding on, he extended his hand and helped him upward. On deck, they were told to chow down and to be ready for the next wave early morning.

Returning to the balkhead where they had spent the evening before, the two began to recall things from their experiences back home.

"Remember Mary Ann Domblosky," asked Gene with a smile.

"Yeh, she beat the heck out of me. I was so embarrassed," he said. "For the first time I knew I could be beaten," he commented with a laugh having a tinge of melancholy. "Those were the days. I still remember the cold weather, the snow, little food. But you know, I don't regret any of it. Look at us now— in good shape, plenty to eat, good clothes, a lot of friends. Tonight we're talking; tomorrow we may be dead. This whole thing is— I don't know what it is. It has to be stupid. I don't know any other word but stupid. War is hell, right, Gene?"

"I know what you mean Rocky," answered Gene as he glanced in the distance toward Iwo Jima where artillery fire lit the skies. "These damned wars! I could never understand them."

"Yeh! The worst part is that we have no choice but to fight and to beat those animals."

"Ya, these damned Japs. They're something else. You know, this ship runs a greater risk of being sunk by one of their suicide planes than by their regular fighters, bombers or artillery fire. Can you imagine the fanaticism of these people? My God!" Gene exclaimed, "these people have given up their minds," he said, not knowing that suicide pilots had already sunk many other ships.

"Given up their minds! What do you mean?" Rocky asked.

"Their thinking is done for them. They ain't got no brain. They have replaced it with what they call courage. What a bunch of fools."

"And we, how about us?" asked Rocky.

"We ain't got it together either. But when I see what's going on in the world, with Germans on the other side and these Japs here, I'd rather be fighting as I am."

The conversation was depressing, the two continuing to talk until they heard word to take cover.

Iwo Jima, they learned from their sergeant, was commanded by Lieutenant General Tadamichi Kiribayashi, who, had made this vow: "Above all, we shall dedicate ourselves and our entire strength to the defense of the island, Iwo Jima!"

With dawn breaking, Rocky and Gene met on top, ready to go ashore. In the distance, rumbles of the battle could be both heard and seen. The waters had finally calmed. The two buddies in full combat gear waited for the order to load.

Again they climbed down the cargo nets, pushing their way for a place in the Higgin's. This time, with the waters being calm, the boat made its way toward the beach head. The closer they got, the louder the explosions became, both from the island and around them. When the boat finally stopped, the marines rushed out screaming under terrifying, ear-shattering artillery fire.

While Rocky was climbing out of the boat, another marine swung his rifle, smacking Rocky across the face. With blood still on his face, Rocky paid little attention to what had happened. When they were ashore, a Medic stopped Rocky.

"Hey, kid!" he said, "Let me see where you got hit."

"I'm not hit; I'm not hit," Rocky said, continuing on.

As they rushed ashore, many fell from enemy fire. The two buddies quickly went their separate ways. Rocky took his position with his team and directed his fire on orders from his Non Commissioned Officer. At one point, the heat from the exploding enemy shells as well as from the firing of his own became very intense. Rocky grabbed a piece of wing from a downed aircraft and used it as a shield. Because of his tendency to want to direct the fire himself, his team buddies began to call him "General Rocky".

"OK, *General Rocky,*" ordered the sergeant, "30 east. Aim and fire."

A smile on his face, young Rocky Castellani quickly obeyed.

"How can you smile in this hell?" yelled the sergeant.

Rocky shrugged his shoulders and went on with his routine, not realizing he had suddenly become a seasoned veteran.

Mount Suribachi

The attack on Mount Suribachi proved decisive in the taking of Iwo Jima. With Colonel Harry B. Liversedge commanding the 28th, the marines, after repelling several bloody counter attacks, succeeded in surrounding and in taking Mount Suribachi. On taking the hill top, the Americans quickly moved to hoist up the flag. On seeing his colleagues boosting up the flag, Rocky became emotional. When the flag began to unfold in the wind, they all responded with resounding cheers of joy.

The flag raising became the symbol of America's will to fight, to endure, and to win. The conquest of Mount Suribachi proved the Americans could take anything and to give back as much if not more.

Shortly after the raising of that flag, an unidentified marine went aboard the beached LST 779 to obtain a larger set of U.S.A. colors. Having gotten a larger one— 96" x 56", the marine moved up the slopes of Suribachi. Associated Press Photographer, Joe Rosenthal, on noticing the incident, immediately followed in close pursuit. When the marine reached the summit, Lieutenant Schrier decided to have the smaller flag lowered and to replace it with the larger one. After a few minutes of work, a group of four men— Sergeant Michael Strand, Corporal Harlon Block, Private First Class Frank R. Sousley, and Private First Class Ira H. Hayes began to hoist the larger flag into the air. Because the flag was large and the wind strong, the four were not able to hold the pole. On seeing the difficulty, Second Class John H. Bradley, a pharmacist, and Private First Class Rene A. Gagnon quickly moved to help. Just as the six marines firmly planted the pole into ground, the Stars and Stripes unfolded to the wind to the joy of Joe Rosenthal, who began to take his historic pictures, and to the rest of the battle-worn marines.

He took 18 photos all together. One of these quickly made history as it was published around the world. Although there was controversy concerning its authenticity, both Mr. Rosenthal and hundreds of eyewitnesses have proven the famous picture was authentic, that it was not posed as some believed.

As it was, the picture became one of the most famous single photos of World War II. It was used as the symbol of the Seventh War Loan Drive, and appeared on literally millions of posters, even on a three cent stamp. It was also to be used to immortalize the marines on Mount Suribachi through the huge bronze statue erected at the Marine Corps War Memorial in Washington, D.C.

Even before mopping-up operations on the slope of Mount Suribachi were completed, plans called for the marines to move to the northern part of the island. Like the drive on Suribachi, the push toward the north began in full earnest. The Japanese, knowing they had their backs to the wall, put on a vicious fight. On both sides, they fell. In that nightmare, death became meaningless amidst the horror of the explosions and the rattling of machine guns. The marines had a tough time advancing— each yard taken measured in blood and death.

Assisted by two other marines, Rocky manned his 60 inch mortar. Suddenly, a shell exploded in his vicinity, killing Frankie, one of his partners, and wounding several others. Unflinching, Rocky pulled to one side and continued with his barrage. When the heat became too intensive, he called for the truck with the water bags to cool down the weapon.

The battle of Iwo Jima went on for many days. Whenever one of his buddies got killed or wounded, Rocky would think back to his father, who had tried so hard to keep him from joining the marines. At night, Rocky spend many hours laying flat on his back. His eyes staring deep into the starry sky, he pictured life in Pennsylvania, his dating Mary, his sisters with their husbands. What contrast! And there he was on the battlefield, manning his weapon, not knowing when to begin firing or being fired upon, not knowing when he would have to kill or be killed.

"Yes, my father was right," he said to himself just as he began to doze off.

"Rocky!" whispered someone. "Where are you?"

It was Lieutenant Bartelli making his rounds to check on the men, to make sure their morale was high. On hearing his name, Rocky identified his position.

"I got good news for you, kid. When we get out of this hell, we're going back to boxing. How are you doing?"

"Except for this mortar which over heats, we're doing fine."

"I heard about your buddies."

"Well, who knows. I may be next."

"Next! Don't talk that way. Remember, you're scheduled to box."

"But right now to fight," Rocky answered, his words full of meaning as though he was an old man near his death and stoically accepting the inevitable.

At that moment, the sky lit up. Bartelli plunged to the ground near Rocky. "This too will pass," he said, raising his voice to compete with the enemy artillery barrage. "Gotta' go check out the other men. Remember what I said, we need you to box for us. See you later," Bartelli said as he crawled away.

Ready for the counter attack, Rocky waited for orders to commence firing. Instead, his platoon sergeant ordered the section to move out to another location. As they stealthily moved around the various positions, they came across another enemy mortar. "That one's mine," yelled Rocky. The sergeant looked at the young marine. Smiling, he granted Rocky's wish.

"When I tell you, fire with all you got."

With the Fifth Division on the left and the Fourth on the right, the Third Division was assigned the task of driving along the relatively flat central portion of Iwo's northern plateau. At 0930 the attack got underway. Initial gains were slight and the losses heavy. However, in their coordinated and relentless attack, using everything from flame throwing tanks to artillery barrages, the marines were able to crack the Japanese line. In two days, they captured the twin hills north of Air Field 2. In a subsequent battle, young Castellani and five other mortar men attacked through the lines of Motoyama Village and seized the hills that dominated Air Field 3.

Hill 382

The biggest and perhaps costliest battle was yet to come. Hill 382 was located in the zone of the Fourth Division. Kuribayashi had turned that hill into a veritable stronghold with all kinds of underground tunnels and gun positions. Its crest had been hollowed out and converted into a huge bunker mounting a lot of artillery pieces and anti tank guns. Dotting the approach were Japanese tanks, carefully hidden in the numerous fissures. Southward of Hill 382 a series of winding ridges and draws terminated in a massive rock called *Turkey Knob*. Further south, there was a natural bowl called the Amphitheater, known to this day as *The Meat Grinder*.

For two weeks, the leathernecks were unable to take that hill, in spite of relentless naval gunfire, artillery and air strikes. An attempt to envelop *Turkey Knob* was thwarted. The marines had to pull back under cover of artillery fire and smoke screen. On the following day the Second Battalion barely managed to get a foothold. The Japanese, however, held on with tenacity.

The attack was repeated the following day. This time, 24 marines of the Second Battalion managed to gain control of Hill 382. *Turkey Knob* and the large *Amphitheater* were not eliminated until the next day.

Hill 362

Up to now, the marines had gone on the offensive only during daylight hours. At night, the Americans held on to their positions, responding fire with fire only if the Japanese fired first. General Erskine, Third Marine Division Commander, decided to take Hill 382 under cover of darkness. On hearing that something different was going to take place, the troops were pleased.

"Whatever it takes to get this damned war over with," Rocky responded.

Before dawn, the troops were instructed to look sharp. The squad leader assembled with his team to go over the attack route. They slowly moved across Iwo's darkened terrain. "Watch your step," whispered the squad leader, on seeing a deep trench to one side. Once in position, the marines opened fire on the unsuspecting Japanese and were able to cross over a heavily defended strip of ground. Demoralized, the Japanese were scattered all over the place, their fighting will all but gone, and their defenses broken. By evening, the marines reached the sea thus consolidating their position.

Mopping up

For the remainder of the campaign, the fighting centered around various pockets of enemy resistance. The Third Marine Division reduced a heavily fortified pocket near Hill 362. The Fourth Division corraled the enemy about halfway between the East Boan Basin and Tachiiwa Point. The Fifth, on the other hand, compressed the Japanese troops into the area around Kitano Point.

The Fourth Sector presented special dangers for the individual marines in that over 300 Japanese held out in deep caves and tunnels with plenty of food, water, and ammunition. Through the use of loudspeakers, the Americans attempted to convince the Japanese to surrender. The psychological warfare did not succeed. Enemy snipers fired from all directions inflicting casualties on the American marines. With the help of flame throwers, grenades and plenty of rifle fire, the Americans finally subdued the stronghold.

The fighting was not by any means over. There were far too many Japanese still willing to fight till the last drop of blood. As the Americans advanced, slowly and painfully, the remaining Japanese were able to re-assemble and fight back. General Kuribayashi's indoctrination had been effective.

Near Kitano Point over 500 seasoned Japanese soldiers, hiding in their defensive positions, were determined to fight and to die in that place. Using two prisoners, General Erskine sent an appeal to surrender. When the Japanese refused, the Americans opened fire.

The conquest of Iwo Jima took a heavy toll. Over 17,000 Americans were wounded and about 6,000 killed. With the island secured, the Americans were able to use the airfields to launch their final attacks onto the nation of Japan.

Reflecting on the manner in which the Americans fought in Iwo Jima, Fleet commander Chester W. Nimitz described the battle in one short sentence:

"Uncommon valor was a common virtue."

Back to Guam

After about 27 days, young Rocky waited on the beach for one of the Higgins Boat to take him on board. As he waited, he was thankful and grateful to be alive, to inhale that salt sea air. He looked around at the scarred surroundings for the last time. Then he marched forward along with hundreds of marines to board the boats that would take them to the troop ship and finally back to Guam. The marines were somber and ecstatic. In their somber moods they thanked God for being alive; in their ecstasy, they exchanged greetings with one another as buddies meet anew.

As the troop ship slid silently through the Pacific, Young Rocky thought he was dreaming, that the past month was simply a nightmare. Looking into the vast Ocean, he thought it was impossible to have gone through that hell, to have seen so much human blood and so much death. As he daydreamed, he thought about boxing and how the sport was going to dominate his life. Resting along the rail, he fell asleep and indeed dreamed about boxing until one of the ship officers awoke him to send him back to his bunk below. Still only seventeen years old, he had seen and lived through ordeals that belied his age.

Second of Seven Championship Fights

Once re-established in tent city, Rocky began to workout as a boxer, making his way around Guam's capital city of Agana. The fighters had their own areas sectioned off. There they trained and waited to gain enough points to be able to go back home to the United States. Rocky figured that he would not have enough points until Christmas time. He could, therefore, go right on and concentrate on his boxing.

With Bartelli, Headquarters scheduled a whole bunch of matches to be held all over the island. After a few months of informal sparring, Bartelli organized a veritable tournament wherein the whole island participated and a championship would be established for each weight division.

In the meantime, Rocky fought around the platoon area, winning prizes such as beer, cigarettes and whiskey, but trading them for Japanese souvenir items. As in the past, it did not take long for him to establish a good rapport with his peers who showed a genuine respect for the young marine.

Three Buddies

With thousands of troops on the island, meeting buddies from home towns was rare indeed. Nevertheless, Rocky had already met up with Gene. Unbeknown to him, two others were stationed in the Tenjo Mountain area, a certain distance from Rocky's tent city near Agana.

Phil Paratore was going through the chow line when he spotted his old pal Red, serving the troop. On recognizing that familiar face, Phil became overjoyed. When Red saw Phil, he reached across the line, hugging and dancing with joy, while the rest of the marines patiently looked on. When the two prolonged their pause, however, some began to complain, ordering Red to get back behind the line to continue to serve. They further complained when they saw that Red had given Phil large portions of food.

"We'll meet at the Recreation Hall tonight," said Red gleefully.

While drinking their beers at the *Rec* Hall, recounting their battle experiences and recalling their lives back home with their friends, they were interrupted by an announcement over the intercom system: Rocky Castellani had just won a bout. Incredulous, Phil jumped to his feet. "Rocky is here; Rocky's here!" he yelled with joy. Red got up and put his arms around Phil, joining him in yelling that Rocky was there. As they swirled around in a long embrace, they lost their

Rocky, Gene Machinist and friends back in Guam.

Rocky with local beauty

equilibrium, finally crashing onto the next table. Apologizing for their fall to the other patrons, the two finally settled down to drinking a few more beers and to make plans on how to go see their buddy, Rocky. The Tenjo Mountain area was under heavy security, and they knew it would take some doing to get passes and transportation to go to Agana.

Next morning, on seeing that Phil was not able to get released, Red, who had pulled some strings, took off with a jeep down the tortuous mountain road.

On locating the training area, Red parked his jeep and rushed into the large tent. Rocky, who was working out, immediately spotted his old buddy. Casting off his gloves, he ran toward Red. Screaming, the two threw their arms around each other as the rest of the fighters looked on with smiles on their faces.

Because a war was still going on, young Rocky knew he just couldn't take off to go see Phil. With Red driving, the two made their way to headquarters, to Lieutenant Bartelli, naturally.

"What's up Rocky?" Bartelli asked, on seeing an excited Rocky such as he had not seen before.

"I need a pass to the Tenjo Mountain to see my friend Phil Paratore."

"I don't know about that. That area is off limits!"

"Off limits? What do I care. Phil is there and I wanna see him. Please get me a pass."

"Just like that?"

"Whatever it takes. Come on, Lieutenant Bartelli, Phil is one of my best buddies."

"Besides," Red interjected, "he's also Italian."

"Come back in a half hour. I'll see what I can do."

After winding their way up the treacherous mountain road, the two finally got to the barracks. Sporting a large cigar he had gotten pursuant to his winning the elimination bout, Rocky walked into the barracks. With Phil nowhere in sight, Rocky headed into the shower area, followed by Red. Sure enough, there was Phil with soap suds all over him. When

Rocky yelled out, Phil turned and, bare as he was, lunged at Rocky.

"You're getting me all wet," Rocky complained, to no avail.

"I'm so happy to see you," Phil muttered repeatedly.

"Ya, yeh, but get the suds off first," Rocky yelled, but making no effort to tear loose from his buddy, except to keep his cigar from getting wet.

After Phil dressed, the three boisterously left the barracks and headed for the Recreational Hall to shoot the bull over a few beers.

"I can't take any more beer," Rocky said when Phil ordered the next round.

"Just like old times, Rocky. You would only go so far. That's why you're so great," Phil commented.

Because Phil and Red had recently joined the service and could not expect to be home for Christmas, they asked Rocky to visit their families, being he stood a good change of getting home by that time.

"If I get home, you can be sure I'll visit all of them. By the way, did you ever run into Mary Jugus?"

"Mary Jugus!" repeated Red. "Who's that?"

"Never mind. She's just a girl I met a long time ago..."

"And..." interrupted Phil.

"And nothing. Just a girl I think I like... What do you guys wanna do tonight?" he asked more to change the subject.

When Rocky learned they were going to be shipped out of Guam, he remembered that Gene Machinist had also been discharged. "When are you guys leaving?" he asked.

"In about a week" Phil answered, with Red agreeing.

"Then you won't be coming to the matches. You know, we're doing very well, and it seems we will get a championship," he said, his enthusiasm measured by the realization that his buddies would be leaving, much as so many of his past buddies. The fact he had seen so many killed made him melancholy.

"Hey, what's up!" exclaimed Red, noticing the mood change in Rocky.

"Nothing, just nothing. We'll have to make sure to write our addresses so we can be in touch."

The Match

Rocky was a Private First Class in the 2nd Battalion Hq. Co., ready to represent the 3rd Marine Division as their only contestant in the Agana Bowl for the All Island Championships. As he stood in his corner, he thought of Phil and Red and how much he had wanted them to be present for the upcoming fight. At that moment, he also thought of home, wishing that at least his relatives might read about him in the papers.

The announcer made his way to the middle of the ring to announce the four round Senior Welterweight Title bout between Rocky Castellani and William King.

Rocky had made up his mind he was going to fight as a boxer rather than a slugger. With that in mind, he moved around the ring, hitting and drawing back, never letting his opponent hit him hard, and never getting caught within the range of King's hard right. As a result, Rocky was able to jab and punch as he had never done before, and in complete control. The bout lasted the full four rounds, with Rocky the winner.

Having wiped his face thoroughly, Rocky was told to approach center ring. "I am happy to announce the new U.S.M.C Senior Welterweight Champ, Attilio *Rocky* Castellani," the Commanding Officer announced to the cheer of the audience. He then turned to Rocky and gave him a medal and a citation. Lieutenant Bartelli almost stood at attention during the ceremony, proud to see his Italian compatriot honored for his boxing accomplishments. Even if one were not aware of the kinship, it would not be difficult to see through Bartelli's smile of how happy and pleased he was. After all, he had been responsible in getting Attilio Castellani into the program.

Unbeknown to him, a month later, the paper of the Wyoming Valley ran a front page story with headlines, "Annexes Island Senior Welterweight Champion!" None of his relatives, including his uncle Michael, read about Rocky, however.

Young Rocky and his buddies were in the chow lines when news broke out that on 7 May 1945 Germany had surrendered. On hearing the news, the marines began to rattle their utensils, to yell and scream fom joy. "The Japs are next!" some screamed. "We're gonna kick the hell out them now," others threatened.

Even Rocky felt a certain excitement about the news, knowing that with additional American forces turning toward the Pacific, the war with Japan had its days numbered. With that thought in mind, he joined his fellow marines in the boisterous celebration. What they did not know was that the U.S. was preparing to end the war once and for all also in the Pacific.

With the dropping of the atomic bomb on Hiroshima and later on Nagasaki in August of 1945, the Japanese finally officially surrendered on the second of September. When the news broke on the island of Guam, the troops went crazy with joy, pandemonium breaking out all over the place. The marines jumped with joy; others knelt in prayer. Rocky, who was working out with his fellow boxers, bowed his head, knowing he had made it after all, and that a new future lay ahead requiring him to make some important decisions.

Home or China

Go back home? Not if he could help it, he finally decided. With the war over, and no longer the risk of being killed, now that he was having the time of his life, he just could not see returning to those cold Pennsylvania winters and to the life he had lived as a youngster. He still remembered the cold in the house, even the lack of food, and the appearance of his father, who too often had to wear W.P.A. clothes. In remembering his mother, he felt a lump in his throat. "I wonder, even if she's dead, if she knows how I feel," he said to himself, as he sat on his bunk, thinking about his decision to stay in the marines. "Mothers should never leave their kids," he thought, remembering the difference in his home after she died, how it affected everyone, especially his sisters.

Having earned the needed points for re-patriation, Rocky began to think of how he could remain in Guam beyond Christmas. As in the past, whenever he had important decisions to make, he would always go see Lieutenant Bartelli.

"I don't wanna go back home," Rocky said while at attention.

"You've got the points and your time is up. I don't think you have much choice," Bartelli answered matter of fact.

"You've gotta find a way out for me. I wanna continue to box for the marines. Isn't there anything along this line? You know I'm pretty good; I'm sure I'll be better. I could tell from the last fight with King. I really learned how to control myself," the new champion said.

"Yes, I could tell. I know you haven't begun yet. You'll be a great boxer, even a world champion if you stick with it, especially if you won't let winning go to your head. You know, a little success often does more harm than good. It's like people who all of a sudden get a little money; it goes to their heads thinking that power through money will get them anything they want," said the ex-great athlete.

"You know I'm not like that. Anyway, I don't wanna' go back home. Will you help me?"

"I'll see what I can do. I'll be in touch with you

soon."

In the next several days, wherever he was, Rocky kept on asking around on how he could remain in the marines, how he could get his orders changed. When he didn't hear from Lieutenant Bartelli, he decided to bring his appeal to his immediate commanding officer. After telling him all about his background, how he grew up in Pennsylvania, when his mother died and how he was living, Rocky pleaded for retention in the marines. "I'll do anything," he said, a tone of deep felt desperation clearly in his voice.

"I don't know what to tell you, Rocky. Regulations are regulations. I don't cut the orders, you know."

"I know, Sir. But you've gotta find a way for me," he pleaded again, his deep brown eyes sad looking.

"Look, Rocky, there isn't anything I can do, unless, unless!"

"Unless what, Sir!" Rocky said, excited.

"Unless your papers got lost. It's happened in the past, many times. In the meantime, you could be transferred to China."

"China?" interrupted Rocky.

"It's probably the only chance you got to stay in the United States Marine Corps. Remember, though, it's a long shot, and you mustn't discuss it with anyone. Understand!" he warned.

"Yes Sir," he answered, his eyes brightening, his forehead full of wrinkles.

"Where there's a will there's a way," commented the Officer in a soft, hardly audible voice.

"What's that Sir?" Rocky quickly asked.

"Nothing, nothing. Just go on with your training. I'm sure you'll hear from us one way or another.

With that, Rocky snapped to attention, released a sharp salute, took one step back, made an about face and marched out of the office, to the delight of his commanding officer.

"He may not know it, but he's got a lot of spunk," the Officer said to himself. With Rocky out of sight, he called his First Sergeant. "I understand Attilio Castellani's papers have been lost."

"Yes Sir," the tough looking First Sergeant answered. "We haven't been able to find them any place."

When he got word that orders had been received that he had been assigned to a special mission to China, Rocky couldn't believe it. Not knowing what he was getting into, and not really caring, he went around to tell his buddies. They all congratulated him for the assignment, with several of them puzzled on how Rocky had been able to pull it off. One even suggested that Bartelli may have been behind it all— after all, he was Italian!

Laying under the hot Guam sun, Rocky stared into the vast blue sky, relaxing from his training, and thinking about back home— the differences in climates, in people, in the way of life, especially his. Not that he felt shame or embarrassment; he simply was choosing something better, and was happy to have the opportunity to have it. When he got up and was gathering his belongings to go back to his quarters, a voice called out to him: "Going to China? You lucky stiff."

Rocky looked up. It was Lieutenant Bartelli.

With the arrangements made, Rocky packed all his belongings, being sure to put his pictures and awards with his other valuables, and moved to the air strip. While the marine airplane was being loaded, Rocky looked around, making sure he would remember that nice, warm place which had given him so much satisfaction and glory, thankful, above all, for having been part of the Guam and Iwo Jima battles and still be whole and alive, unlike so many of his fellow marines and buddies.

Chapter 10

Mission to China

From Guam, Rocky flew directly to Tsingtao, China. On arriving, the first thing that hit him was the cold weather, which was worse than that of his home town. In the land of the notorious *War Lord* Chiang Kai-shek, Rocky was to learn that his new tour of duty was not going to be the greatest in the world. Because he was so young, and in spite of his mature behavior, he nevertheless made easy comparison between places, especially between the warm beaches of Guam and the desolate cold terrain of China.

New Year's Eve
"I wished I had never heard of China and the Chinese!" he said to himself on discovering he was guarding a heap of coal. Freezing to death, he walked around that place in the middle of China, with a rifle on his shoulder, worrying whether the Mongolyians would come down on him to rob that black coal. "A far cry from boxing," he bitterly told himself. "Well, what can you do. I goofed," he continued in a silent soliloquy. "But, I gotta keep warm or else I'll die. And who the hell wants to die in this hell hole!"

To keep warm, Rocky took the rifle off his shoulder and began to shadow box. He moved around, dancing

Rocky in China

from place to place. Except for the wind which broke the deadly silence of the night, Rocky did his best to keep his punches silent; for, he did not want anyone to hear him.

Unexpectedly, the guard officer appeared from behind. Seeing Rocky dancing in earnest, he stopped to pause. Certainly, he did not know if Rocky was dancing or had simply gone crazy. After a few moments, he walked forward. On seeing him, Rocky quickly went for his rifle.

"Halt, who goes there!" he yelled in a loud voice.

"Guard Officer."

"Advance to be recognized!"

"Good job Castellani... Now, will you tell me what the hell you were doing?"

Rocky explained he was cold and thought of keeping warm by shadow boxing. "I used to do that in Pennsylvania when it was cold."

"You're not in Pennsylvania. And you're not dealing with Americans. You're dealing with Mongolyians here. They're apt to come down any time for this coal. They've been known to kill. So, you had better stay sharp and keep your eyes open. Understand!"

"Yes Sir!" the young marine answered.

"Now, what about this boxing?" the officer inquired, smiling.

"Boxing?" Rocky repeated, surprised about the manner in which the marine officer had put it. "What do you mean, sir?" he asked, his eyes bright.

"I know you've done a good amount of boxing. Would you be interested in joining the boxing team up in Tientsin, North China?"

Rocky had accepted the tour in China to avoid going home to an uncertain future; but he hadn't figured on going to China to guard coal. He had stayed in the marines with the hope to continue to box— to learn the sport and to get paid at the same time, and to be sure about his next meal. On hearing the offer to box, he quickly told the Officer all about his boxing career, especially the last competition on Guam, that if he wanted to see the medals and all the other awards he had received, he would be happy to show them...

"Stop, Castellani, you don't have to tell me more or show me anything. We know all about you."

"You do?" the kid said, smiling.

"Come see me in the morning. And, walk your post according to instructions. No shadow boxing here; you'll have plenty of chances for the real thing."

"Yes sir!" Rocky answered, smartly bringing his rifle to present arms.

When the Officer was out of sight, Rocky jumped into the air screaming, "Happy New Year!"

Rocky, like so many of his peers, simply could not understand that those coal shipments were vital to the Chinese people whose land was still partially under Japanese invading forces. As General Wedemeyer pointed out to his Third Amphibious Corps, which operated in the Tientsin region, without that coal the public facilities and factories would stop operating; thus, thousands of people would starve and cause social upheavals. At the level of the enlisted men, issues or ideas of "vital" or non "vital interest", that the people of China might have had for the United States, was not paramount. For Rocky, boxing was all encompassing, and the struggle for survival, now that he was assured of his next meal, was a thing of the past.

Ubaldo Giometti

In a few days, Rocky was packed, ready to go to Tientsin. Together with a marine Second Lieutenant, the two rode their jeep through some 60 miles of the roughest roads ever until they got to Tientsin.

Assigned a barrack, with the usual rack and locker, Rocky was now at home in what looked like more of the same— cold weather and people whom he neither recognized nor understood. That would soon change, however.

Paying little attention to the people around him, Rocky concentrated on his boxing, on his being and getting in shape, giving it all he had. In the several preliminary bouts before the February Championship Night Fights, he did very well, winning all the encounters except for one. In that scrap, Rocky received a good sound beating from a brawling and powerful marine. Undaunted, Rocky continued to train and to meet other challengers as though he had never had a fight before that one.

These qualities caught the eye of Ubaldo Giometti, an Italian national who had been China's undefeated light heavyweight champion for nine years. A veteran of the Japanese occupation of northern China, he remained in Tientsin where he was asked by the U.S. Armed forces to help train the boxing team.

"Attilio Castellani?" Ubaldo said, pronouncing Rocky's name in Italian. *"Ma tu sei italiano...* Are you Italian?"

"Si, sono italiano... Yes, I'm Italian, but I was born in America, Pennsylvania. But, what's an Italian doing here?"

"Parliamo in italiano, ti dispiace... Do you mind if we speak in Italian. I haven't spoken Italian for so many years. I've been watching you. You're pretty good. You've got a lot to learn, but you're pretty good. I'd be happy to work with you if you wish," Ubaldo said in haulting Italian.

"Va bene... Great!" answered Rocky. "I prefer to speak English. I practically forgotten the Italian I learned from my parents."

"O.K., we'll speak English, but I miss speaking Italian. Besides, my English is not too good. Look, I will speak to the Officer in Charge of the Tournament to see if I can be your trainer. *Va bene...* Alright?"

"Alright!... *Va bene!...* Of course," Rocky answered without hesitation. His eyes were bright, a wide smile on his face. *"Va bene... va bene,"* he repeated enthusiastically. "And, I'll teach you to speak very good Italian, okay?"

Mr. Giometti would also be the trainer of Frenchy La Salle, a lightweight. Together with his promising boxers, Ubaldo took them to the dispensary for a medical check.

"*Ciao bella...* Hi, beautiful," Ubaldo greeted the young nurse.

"You again. What can I help you with this time?" she answered matter-of-fact.

"I'm here for these two boys; they need a medical check up."

"Oh," she said, raising her head, her eyes fixed on Rocky. "What's your name?"

"Rocky... Attilio Castellani."

"Rocky? Oh, yes. You're the boy wonder of boxing... My name's Betty. We'll be taking care of your health needs."

The marine officer in charge of the U.S.A. Marine Corps Amateur Boxing Championship Night of February 3, 1946 wanted the evening to be unforgettable. He scheduled the event in the 17,000 seat Hai Alai Club Auditorium. A second tournament was scheduled in Shanghai at a later date.

In the eliminations, young Rocky fought several bouts, winning them all, three by TKO, thus assuring himself a spot in the finals. He fought people like Sal Fontana, Danny Bucci, and Charlie Sterner. In every encounter, Rocky finished on top both as a boxer and as a young man with dignity. The successes did not go to his head. He was still the unassuming, somewhat withdrawn young man he had always been, a characteristic that made him likable to many people, including his peers and Betty. She asked Ubaldo all kinds of questions.

"*La ragazza ti vuole bene...* The girl likes you," Ubaldo said.

"That's good," Rocky answered.

"Is that all you can say?" Giometti asked.

"I'm here to box. I don't mix much."

"E va bene... If that's what you want."

Wearing the marine colors of red and gold, Giometti's boxers fought well. With a hard left followed by a right hook, Frenchy La Salle knocked out George Hines of North Carolina. Rocky, on the other hand, was not as lucky. Sammy Muscato of New York proved to be a tougher opponent. No matter how hard Rocky tried to knock him down, Sammy just would not budge. Nevertheless, Rocky won the fight by a close decision.

General Tu Shien Shih, Deputy Mayor of Tientsin, awarded Silver Cups to the winners— symbolic of Chinese-American good will. Pfc. Joseph M. Pavlak, USMC reporter, recorded the historic evening with a complete description of the other awards and picture ceremonies that took place, his articles appearing in many newspapers throughout the world.

US Marine Corps General De Witt Peck, Commanding Officer of the First Marine Division, presented *Young Rocky* Attilio Castellani with a championship award and the *Silver Buckle Belt Award,* indicating he was the Pacific Ocean Area Middleweight Champion. Obviously pleased, Rocky accepted the awards with pride.

With the excuse of wanting to make sure he was not hurt, Betty made her way to the ring. When Rocky stepped down to go to the dressing quarters, she approached him.

"We're celebrating at the Rec. Will you be coming?"

"I guess so," he answered half-heartedly.

As usual, the kid took his shower and went back to the barrack. Flat on his back, he stared at the ceiling. With the images of his mother and sisters flashing by, he soon fell asleep, oblivious of the festivities around him.

Betty, who celebrated with Ubaldo, Frenchy and many others, liked Rocky very much. She was attracted to him both for his quite manner and his good wholesome looks, and was unhappy on being rejected, especially when so many other men wanted her.

"I'm not rejecting you," Rocky explained a few days later, while walking down a crowded Chinese street. "I haven't been spending time with any girls, that's all."

While the two were talking, a black limousine with flags on the front bumper appeared from down the street. It was the car of Chiang Kai-shek.

"Who's that?" Rocky asked, absorbed by the sight.

"It looks like Chiang Kai-shek. He comes around these areas very often," Betty explained.

Seized by an unexplainable urge, Rocky dashed down the street toward the car, which had come to a stop. He rushed in front, removed one of the flags and ran all the way back to the USMC area as fast as he could. On reaching his bunk, he threw himself on it. He had gotten his prized Chinese trophy and wasn't going to give it up. "Chiang Kai-shek's flag? I can't believe it!"

"What made you do that silly thing?" she asked in a perturbed tone, a few days later.

"I don't know. I just wanted to take something back as a souvenir. I guess I like flags... You know, come to think of it, that was stupid. I'm sorry."

On their next tour downtown, Betty made sure Rocky would not repeat the prank with the flag, assuring him that if he had gotten away with it the first time, the second might prove fatal. She knew a lot about Chinese culture and much more about the people, especially those in power.

"We just can't do the things we are apt to do in the States. A lot of the things we do there are taken as offenses here. Do you understand?"

"Sure. How about just going around looking at the Pagodas. You know, I like those things."

Rocky, Ubaldo and Frenchie

"Of course you would. You're Italian."

"Ya, but what has that got to do with anything."

"Italians are great artists. There's art in every Italian," she confirmed. When she saw Rocky frown and shrugging his shoulders, she added: "You don't think so?"

"Sure I do, sure," he repeated.

Toward the end of their sightseeing tour through the vast crowds and congested streets and buildings, the two returned to the military base. Betty put her arms around Rocky to kiss him. When she felt a certain resistance on his part, she released her grip. "What's the matter, you don't like me?" she mildly complained.

"Of course I like you. The problem is that I don't want to like you. I've got to like boxing before anything else," he said in a serious voice.

Convinced about his seriousness, Betty tightened her arms around him again, bringing her mouth to his and kissing him, first gently, then with passion, not caring he did not kiss back with the same intensity. When she pulled back from her kiss, she stared into his eyes. "What a waste," she commented, a sad expression on her face. "Here we are, we could be making some real wonderful love, and you don't even know what I'm talking about."

"I told you, I haven't been spending time out with girls."

"I can tell. But you needn't apologize. Maybe that's why I like you so much. I could teach you," she said with hesitation, knowing she was talking above his head as far as the meaning of love was concerned. "That's all right," she said, being sure she was neither patronizing him nor belittling him. "I really like you, Rocky Castellani. You are special!"

The United States Navy Seventh Fleet had scheduled its boxing tournament February 14 in Shanghai in a huge auditorium. Word had gotten around on the toughness of the Marine Tientsin Boxing Team. For this reason, the marines became feared. When they arrived in Shanghai, they were told the team could not participate because the tournament was for Navy boxers only.

"Wait a second," injected Rocky, who had been patiently waiting around the desk of the knit-picking Navy promoter. "Do you know who pays us?"

"What does that mean?" the rotund promoter asked.

"We get paid by the Navy. So, we're Navy and we're here to fight in the tournament. We haven't traveled all this distance from Tientsin just to come look at your boys fight," he said, causing his colleagues to look up and to nod with approval.

"Yeh," interjected one, "my check is a Navy check."

"All right, all right!" the promoter said. "Wait here. Let me see what I can do. I'll be right back."

"Bravo!" Ubaldo said, patting Rocky on the shoulder.

Needless to say, the marines were allowed to participate in the Pacific Fleet Ring Title Fights.

During the elimination bouts, Joe Girard tagged Rocky on the chin, sending him down for an eight count. Rocky, however, was able to come back and win by a decision. For the middleweight bout, Rocky had to face a Pittsburgh, Pennsylvania boxer by the name of Stepanovich, a big and rugged one hundred and sixty-two pounder.

Remembering the close call he had had with Girard, Rocky decided to train extra hard for the championship bout. With Ubaldo giving him instructions, Rocky ran his usual five miles; this time, however, harder and in more earnest. Before the bout, he made sure to eat and to relax. The latter was hard to come by, however.

"What's the matter Rocky?" Ubaldo asked, noticing Rocky was anxious.

"I don't know. I think I'm a bit nervous."

"Don't worry. You'll be fine. Here, let's go over some points..."

With approximately 50,000 boxing fans in attendance, the night was electrifying. On entering the ring, Rocky felt exhilarated from the tremendous cheers from the crowd, proud to wear the Marine Corps colors and knowing he was going to win.

A reporter covering the evening, was so impressed that he described the bout between Rocky Castellani and Red Stepanovich as follows: "The best mill of the evening came when Rocky Castellani faced Red Stepanovich of Tsingtao in the middleweight class. The former won the fight in which both men put on a magnificent performance. Head ducked down, Castellani charged like a bull into his opponent, landing rights and lefts, took the first round. The third round saw Stepanovich fight with renewed zeal but his stamina was fast wearing out. Castellani won a well-deserved victory in the best scrap of the night..."

The "scrap" created a lot of excitement with the interservice spectators, especially among the high ranking officers and Chinese officials, who were extremely pleased. They cheered when Rear Admiral Walter F. Boone stepped into the ring to congratulate Rocky for his tremendous victory, and to crown him the Pacific Fleet Ring Middleweight Title Champion.

That evening, there was a huge party given on behalf of the participants. As usual, Rocky remained quiet, drinking his beer, eating his food, and generally happy over the attention he was receiving. Ubaldo, on the other hand, more than made up for Rocky in celebrating. He had gotten some Italian wine and was sharing drinks with just about all the people around him, including the ranking Chinese officials.

"Rocky, come on! You too. Take a glass and drink with us."

A smile on his face, Rocky obliged, to the cheers of his friends and admirers. When Ubaldo tried to refill the glass, Rocky refused. "I know," he said, "you wish Betty were here, don't you?" Ubaldo chided with a smirk.

"Betty? Oh, yes. I think you'd like her to be here."

"Si, Attilio, amico mio... Yes, Attilio my friend. And just because she isn't here, doesn't mean there aren't others. We got some Chinese girls. What do you say? You want to come?"

Rocky looked at him, smiled and nodded in the negative. What Ubaldo could not know was that Rocky was thinking about Mary Jugus and about his sisters and father. And what Rocky did not know was that his name would make the local papers.

Leaving China

Back in Tientsin, Betty arranged a small party on behalf of Rocky to celebrate the victory. With Ubaldo, Lenny and a few others, Betty served Chinese delicacies. She had even gotten wine from Ubaldo, who, as usual, was the life of the party, entertaining everyone with his broken English.

"How come you and Rocky are so different?" Betty asked. "Both of you are Italian," she observed.

"Us, Italians?" Ubaldo questioned. "Rocky is not Italian. If he was..."

"If he *were...*" she interrupted with a smile.

"If he were," he repeated with a laugh, "he would have made love to you."

"You're so sure of yourself."

"Need you say it," he answered in straight English. "In any event, seriously speaking, Italian Americans are Americans. Besides boxing, I've been teaching Rocky Italian. They know so little about Italy. If they *were* Italians, do you think Italy would have declared war on the United States? Except for the immigrants, who remain with fixed memories, the Italian American is not Italian."

"I don't know about that. Besides, you've never been in America."

"I know, but I've seen many like Rocky around here."

"I like you both, and both of you are Italians," she said with a smirk. "Too bad Rocky is leaving. I think in due time he'd come around. He's so clean looking and healthy. There are times when we women really look for that. Unfortunately, there aren't too many around. Most are just like you."

"Like me," he commented, his eyes opening wide. "We'll see you later then?"

"Si, amore," she said in a low voice.

"You learn fast. To our health," he said, lifting his glass of wine. Then, looking at Rocky, he got the group to drink a toast: "To Attilio Castellani— Young Rocky— may you become the World Middleweight Champion, because we are already so very proud of you. You're going to be a great professional. I know you will."

By evening's end, the nurse approached Rocky. "So you're leaving. Except for boxing, you've been a fool," she said with a half smile which hid some bitterness.

"What's that?" Rocky asked.

"Oh, never mind. Here, just kiss me." She moved toward him and kissed him passionately. "I'm sorry. I'm the fool," she said between kisses.

Lieutenant Snow was in charge of recruiting. His job was to encourage as many enlisted men to stay on in the Marine Corps.

"If you enlist you'll make sergeant. I promise you."

"No thanks," Rocky answered respectfully. "My mind's made up. If I want to do anything with boxing, I have to do it where it counts, out there."

"I guess you're right," Lt. Snow commented, impressed by the seriousness of the young marine. "If you don't want to re-enlist, go home and become a pro. If you do good, great! If not, you can always return and re-enlist for two more years in the U.S.M.C.. Of course, I'd love to see you go to France and fight Marcel Cerdan for the world title." Snow was referring to a probable inter-service world title fight— Army against the Marine Corps, which did not materialize because Rocky decided to take his honorable discharge.

On leaving Lt. Snow, Rocky ran into Lenny Ziolinski, who was next in line for the re-up talk. "I guess we'll be getting out together," Lenny commented. "Maybe we'll be on the same ship together. I'll be in touch," Lenny said to Rocky, who was apparently pleased over that possibility.

With his memorabilia and personal belongings safely packed, Rocky mustered out of the China Theater of War Area, heading for Camp Pendleton, California.

Chapter 11

Return to Pennsylvania

Unofficially out of the U.S.M.C., and only still eighteen years old, for the first time in his life Rocky had a few dollars in his pocket, new clothes, many new friends like Lenny, with whom he was traveling, and glad to be alive.

After leaving Camp Pendleton, the two took the train to the Chicago Marine Transient Station where they were officially discharged. On looking out the train on their last leg toward home, Rocky thought about the Wyoming Valley's coal fields, the smoke and soot, the black, gray and dirty looking cities, and wondered if he had made the right decision to go back home.

"You know, Lenny, when I think about the coal mines, I wonder if I shouldn't have stayed in the marines."

"Wait till you start boxing as a pro. You won't want to get back in the military. I assure you."

"I know, but at times I wonder," young Rocky said.

"Forget it," Lenny assured. "We'll soon be at my house. My mother is waiting. I'm sure you'll like her. She's a good cook and I know you like to eat."

After many hours on the tiresome train, the two arrived in Pittsburgh early in the morning. After joyously embracing her son and Rocky, Mrs. Ziolinski prepared a hearty breakfast. The two ate till they could no more.

"I know you're tired," Mrs. Ziolinski said. "I got the beds ready. You can go take a nap. I'll wake you up when your dad gets back. By that time the rest will be here. Oh, I'm so glad to have you back home!"

While the two slept, Mrs. Ziolinski quitely prepared a special evening meal for the whole family. When Mr. Ziolinski arrived at about five o'clock, the two marines were still sleeping.

"He's in bed," Mrs. Ziolinski answered.

"Well, get him up," he said firmly. "I want to see him."

Rocky enjoyed the attention he was receiving from the Ziolinski family. He particularly enjoyed the food, just as Lenny had predicted. On seeing Lenny seated next to his mother, who kept on putting her arms around her son, Rocky became pensive. Mrs. Ziolinski noticed the change and went over to Rocky.

"Everything alright, Rocky?" she said, putting her hand on his shoulder. "Can I get you something else?"

"No thanks, Mrs. Ziolinski. I'm fine."

"Are you having a good time?"

"Marvelous!" he responded vivaciously. Although her homemade cooking made him feel good, he thought an awful lot about his mother Rose, and wondered what it was going to be like back home with his dad and sisters after having been away for so long.

"Lenny tells me you're going to be a boxer," Mr. Ziolinski asked. "We hope Lenny will go into politics instead."

"Dad," interrupted Lenny, "Rocky is a very good fighter. He'll have to send us tickets when he meets for the world title."

"Is that a promise?" asked Mr. Ziolinski with a great grin.

"I'll do my best. That I can assure you."

At the bus station the next morning, before getting

146

on, Rocky thanked Lenny for his friendship. "I had fun. Now it's time to go see if I can fight with the pros.!" He shook Lenny's hand, then wrapped his arms around his buddy and got on the bus for his eight hour trip through Harrisburgh, and east through the rolling green springtime hills of Northeastern Pennsylvania.

On arriving in the Wyoming Valley, late in the afternoon, he looked across Wilkes Barre city square, his eyes poised on the second floor windows of Mr. Al Flora's boxing gymnasium. After putting his duffel bag in a bus terminal locker, he headed toward the gym. He looked around, inspecting the quarters, and was pleased to see what there was. Then, as he was about to go back to the terminal, he ran into a couple of his old buddies, who enthusiastically began to ask him all sorts of questions about the war.

"I haven't been home yet. We'll talk about it tonight. What? we'll be meeting here around nine?"

He got his gear and took a bus across the Market Street, Kingston Bridge to his father's house at 618 North Street, Luzerne.

He had never written to his father, and his father had never written to him. Except for some CARE packages he received, he knew very little about his family. He didn't know his father had re-married to an Italian woman by the name of Connie, who had a daughter and two adopted boys, Tony, Angelo, and and older son Birtch.

With his duffel bag on his shoulder, Rocky walked up the stairs, put the bag down and paused for a moment before knocking, wondering if anyone was home as there was no sign of life inside. When he finally knocked, Yolanda appeared at the door. Surprised, she immediately put her arms around him, kissing him on the face several times. Rocky wrapped his arms around her waist, tears dropping down his face.

"I'm so happy, I'm so happy," she repeated frantically. "I'm so happy you're back."

"Where is every body?" he asked, as he pushed her forward so as he could better look into her face and eyes. "My, you're pretty?"

Slightly blushing but still exuberant, Yolanda took her brother into the kitchen where she told him to sit down. While she prepared some sandwiches, she gave him a full report on the family. "But you know, our father is very sick. He's still got that Sellicosis and he's now at the doctor's for a check up."

The two had hardly begun telling each other their stories when the new Mrs. Castellani— Connie, appeared with the two boys. On seeing her, Yolanda quickly made the introduction, in Italian, being that Connie spoke very little English. On hearing Rocky answer her in good Italian, she was surprised. When he told her about Ubaldo in China and how they spoke Italian, she was even more amazed. Meanwhile, the two boys hung close to Rocky, looking him over, often staring at him for prolonged periods of time.

"See how they admire you," Yolanda said proudly, bringing a smile from Rocky.

Connie was a simple, down to earth woman. She took a liking to Rocky and told him so. She turned to Yolanda and told her to go easy on the sandwiches.

"Preparo io da mangiare... I'll prepare dinner. You just entertain your brother until your father comes home. You go to the other room and leave the kitchen to me."

While Rocky was spreading out his memorabilia, being extra careful with the trophies, medals and certificates, Mr. Castellani appeared at the door.

"Papa!" exclaimed Yolanda.

"Attilio!" exclaimed Mr. Castellani. He rushed to his son and both embraced. *"Quando sei arrivato...* When did you arrive?"

"Poco fa... A while ago. I'm happy to be home. I met your new wife, and I like these two little ones. How are you? They told me you were at the doctor.

What's he saying?

"Bene! Tutto bene. Good, all good... Connie!" he yelled, *"stai preparando da mangiare...* are you preparing dinner?" he asked, avoiding having to answer his son about his frail health, even though the doctor had seemed optimistic.

"Look pop!" Rocky said proudly, "these are all the things I won in the marines... in China. I became a champion. See this belt... I said I was going to be a champion boxer!"

Mr. Castellani scrutinized the memorabilia, apparently happy about his son's successes. Above all, he was happy to have him home and alive, even though they hadn't written to each other.

"What you got in the bag?" asked Tony.

"Can you show us?" asked Angelo.

Rocky obliged by taking out his uniform and the rest of his belongings. When Mr. Castellani saw the uniform with the stripes and the brass, he asked his son to put it on. *"Voglio vederti in divisa militare...* I want to see you in your military uniform. Please!" he asked, while the two boys cheered and Yolanda made her usual comments of approval.

In a few minutes, Rocky re-appeared. "Madonna!" exclaimed Yolanda, with the kids making their own comments. But it was Mr. Castellani, who was really proud to see his son standing tall and looking so good. He remembered when he was in the Italian Army, when he wore the uniform: it always made him feel different— more important. But there was no comparison between how his son looked then and now. "Connie!" he called out to his wife, *"vieni a vedere...* come see! And he isn't nineteen years old yet."

Chapter 12

Turning Professional

Rested and happy, the next morning after having had breakfast with Yolanda, Rocky made his way across the square up to Mr. Flora's Gym. He walked up the steps and out onto the workout area. Looking at the empty ring, he wondered how to go about becoming a pro fighter: was he to tell whoever was in charge that he was there, that he was experienced, that he was a Marine Champion? Would he have to give a test to show his boxing skills?

A test? That was the answer: prove himself by boxing and not by talking. Unexpectedly, the opportunity came. While standing in front of the ring, two boxers climbed through the ropes followed by Joe Rodona, an interested friend of Mr. Flora. After a few minutes, one of the boxers who had been noticing the intensity with which Rocky was following their sparring, stopped and asked Rocky if he wanted to get into the ring.

"Of course," Rocky answered without hesitation, getting the attention of Joe Rodona, who looked at Rocky's build and sensing that this young man was not just a bystander. Without giving the boxer the chance to change his mind, Rocky quickly asked Joe Rodona for a pair of shorts and gloves.

"I'll ask Frankie," Joe answered with a slight hesitation, knowing that Frankie Cardanelli was in the dressing room waiting to do some sparring, but not having anyone. "I don't know about this," Joe said to himself while walking toward the dressing room to talk to Frankie. In a minute or so, Joe called Rocky over to talk with Frankie.

After Rocky explained that he knew how to fight, that he wanted to be a pro fighter, Frankie agreed to enter the ring with the *kid*. Meanwhile, Joe Rodona wondered if he had made a mistake in getting his boxer involved like that.

Having gone through the first round just dancing and figuring out his opponent, Rocky decided to show what he was made of in the second round. He plowed into Frankie, who answered in kind. When Rocky began to get the better of the pro, Joe stepped into the ring. "You're supposed to be sparring not fighting," he said to Rocky. "I'm calling it quits for today."

Not knowing whether or not to be disappointed, Rocky left the gym to wander through the city to see if he could meet with some of his old buddies, wondering about Red and Phil. Meanwhile, Joe went to see Mr. Flora to tell him about Rocky.

Al Flora, May 6, 1946

Pursuant to a message left at home, next morning Rocky made his way again to the gym to speak with Mr. Flora.

"You're Rocky, the marine," Mr. Flora said, a smile on his face.

"Yes sir," quickly responded Rocky, causing Flora to raise his eyebrows.

"Very good. Tell me about your boxing in the marines. We read a little bit about you."

To Flora's delight, Rocky told him about his having been boxing on Guam, how he had won championships in Guam and China, and how much he wanted to turn pro because he was confident about his boxing abilities. Impressed, Flora proposed to give Rocky some time to show whether he truly had it. If he proved himself, Flora would agree to be his trainer and manager.

"Is that agreeable with you?" Flora asked.

"Yes sir!" responded Rocky. "When do we start?"

"You start tonight: in bed by nine, up by five. In the meantime, you run, you rest, you walk, you eat, you sleep. Above all, you workout. If you think you can handle this rigid fighter's schedule, I will train and manage you. But you have to do these things faith- fully. No slacking off!" While they were standing there, Al Flora commented to Rocky he had fought his cousin Michael Costello years ago.

Young Rocky Castellani found his old buddies, Phil Paratore, Red, and the Machinist brothers more than just helpful. In fact, they gave him a heck of a 19th birthday party. For the next three months, they assisted him in the training, often going with him to and from Bunker Hill. Meanwhile, Flora scheduled the first fight to be held on August 15 against a proven fighter by the name of Johnny Stoffy. To be on the safe side, Flora made it a four round preliminary bout to be held at the Scranton Youth Center which had a seating capacity for only a few hundred fans. He instructed Joe Rodona and Frankie Cardanelli to work with Rocky to prepare him for this very important first victory.

Although Rocky maintained his regimen, he found time to buy a used car, to go visit Father Dolan and later took gifts to the Sisters' Convent on Washington Street. He was, afterall, receiving a monthly check from the USMC, which gave him the kind of financial stability he needed during this transition. He felt good about that security, but never forgot he was the son of a poor coal miner struggling to make ends meet.

On driving through the square, Rocky saw Mary standing at the bus stop. On seeing her, he stopped. It was midnight, and Mary had just gotten off work.

"Hi Mary, can I give you a lift home?" he asked gently. When she did not respond (afterall, she didn't really know him), Rocky explained who he was and that he had been over her house.

"Sure," she then answered. "But I'm going right home. My mother always waits for me at the bus stop."

On the way, Rocky told her about himself— the things he had done in the marines, and how he was turning professional, that he was taking some courses in the evening adult education division, and that above all, he wanted to date her from time to time. To the latter, Mary answered that she had to see.

"That's fine. I'll stop at your house from time to time. If I see you here at the bus stop, I'll give you a ride. Then if you like me, we can go out."

Mrs. Jugus was waiting at the bus stop. Rocky stopped the car. "Mrs. Jugus, remember me? I'm Attilio. I just saw Mary waiting for the bus and I gave her a ride home. Come in, I'll take you both home."

"His name is *Rocky* now," interjected Mary.

Surprised, Mrs. Jugus shrugged her shoulders. Without saying a word, she got into the car. "Young Rocky!" she exclaimed, a smile on her face, pleased by Rocky's manner as well as by his appearance, even though she didn't really like Italians.

One of the great things Al Flora did was to assign many young amateurs to spar with Rocky, so he could get used to many styles of fighting, and to learn how to cope with the erratic ones.

Joe Rodona worked hard with the kid through May, June, July and August. He made the proper moves, talked with Flora, adjusted the training routine and did whatever needed be done to make it easy for Rocky. Even Frankie Cardanelli gave of his time and expertise.

Third on a card of six fights, the evening of August

15 was unusually hot. For Rocky, the four round bout was also the first real match since leaving the marines. What went through his mind, while waiting in the locker room, was that he was not going to lose.

With that determination, he entered the ring. As he looked into the audience, he noticed his father sitting ringside, with an obvious proud expression on his face. Rocky waved to him, and Mr. Castellani waved back, the words *"buona fortuna... good luck"* on his lips.

Johnny Stoffy was introduced first. When the announcer introduced Rocky as the former Marine Champion and Pride of the marines, the crowd gave a thunderous reception.

The fight went Rocky's way from the first round. In the fourth, knowing he had won thus far, Rocky decided to show the crowd he had much more. To their joy, Rocky moved to one side of Johnny. Then, with lightening speed, he caught Johnny on the chin for the full count.

Al, Frankie and Joey were thrilled beyond words. They figured the kid was pretty good; a kayo the first time out was more than they had hoped. As a result, they celebrated the victory late into the night until Rocky asked to be taken home.

Sunday morning, Al Flora took Rocky to church. Before and after services, he saw how people gravitated towards the kid and how nice they were to him. What was good was that *Young* Rocky had natural charisma and did not know it. Flora, who had noticed that quality, now knew a star was about to be born.

Flora did not waste time. He scheduled a second bout for August 30 in the Hazelton Ball Park in Hazleton, with Joe Kiddish. The evening was hot, and so was Rocky, who took the four round bout with ease. On the third of September, Flora had Rocky meet Billy Brown in Scranton in a six rounder. Wearing the Marine Corps colors, and with Mr. Castellani ringside, Rocky won by decision. Because Billy Brown's promoter challenged Rocky for a second bout, Flora conceded, scheduling another six rounder in the Wilkes Barre Armory for September 26. With a few sports reporter predicting Rocky would hit the canvass for the first time, Rocky went into the ring more determined than ever. He had to prove himself, and knew he had to floor his opponent rather than being floored. In the fourth round, just as he done in his first fight, Rocky caught Billy on the chin and send him down for the full count, to a pandemoniously rejoicing crowd.

For his next opponent, Flora signed with Stan Miller, a clever fighter who not only was good, but was also young and eager. With this match, Flora hoped to convince the press about Castellani being a serious fighter. Though the bout was another six rounder, Flora placed it first before the main one. Predictably, Rocky floored Stan in the last round. The Wattras Armory crowd was so pleased they gave him a standing ovation.

Pete Fulton

Aside from the reporters, who were finally convinced, Mr. Pete Fulton, the Produce King from Wilkes Barre, got interested in Rocky. After talking with Al Flora, Pete got 20% of the kid's action which was now split three ways.

A nice guy, Pete Fuller liked Attilio from the first moment. In fact, he asked Rocky to move into his home so as he could better concentrate on his boxing. By Thanksgiving, Rocky moved in with Mr. and Mrs. Fulton. Flora quickly scheduled a six rounder with the feared Stan Perrock for November 6 in Wilkes Barre's Kingston Armory. With Mr. Castellani, Father Dolan, uncle Mike and Phil in the audience, Rocky caught Stan on the chin and send him to the canvass in the third. Needless to say, the crowd went wild. In the locker room, and in the presence of his trainers and Mr. Castellani, Father Dolan gave his congratulations.

First Main Bout

With the crowd and press wondering whether Rocky could keep up that pace, Al and Pete, who by now had gotten to know their boxer really well, scheduled Rocky to fight Billy Kilroy on November 26 in the big Wattras Armory. Unlike his recent bouts, this time Rocky trained extra hard. He worked out of Al's gym and ran up to Bunker Hill on a regular basis, knowing he had to be as good for the first main event as he was for his first bout as a pro. On seeing their boxer train in earnest, the men around him weren't worried, knowing he would win.

During the second round, however, Billy caught Rocky on the left eye causing a rather large gash. When the referee saw it bleed profusely, he quickly stopped the fight and asked the Doctor for an opinion. With the Doctor giving the go ahead, Rocky continued. In the fourth, when Frankie Cardanelli realized Rocky could not see with his eye, he called out to the referee to stop the fight. Sad but confident, Rocky went to the hospital where he was sewn up, then to his home where he went to bed and slept like a baby.

Remembering he had been scheduled for another bout with Beau Jack January 13th of the new year, Rocky passed the holidays with his family at his father's house. With Connie taking the lead, the women went out of their way to make that Christmas a real memorable one. Mary, Anne and their respective husbands all arrived early in the morning. Uncle Mike and his family arrived just before the meal. Needless to say, Rocky was busy with the kids who gave him no rest, much to his pleasure.

With Connie giving the meal's prayer in Italian, they sat to enjoy a rather opulent meal made up of practically all types of home made specialties: pasta, meats, vegetables, desserts, etc.

"Is it okay if I still call you uncle Mike, Michael?"

157

Rocky jokengly asked, causing everyone to laugh.

"Attilio?" asked uncle Mike on seeing him pensive during the prayer. "What are you thinking about?"

"Just a thought about my mother. I wish she were here," he said softly, a lump in his throat. Yolanda, who was sitting next to him, brought her hand to his shoulder.

After the meal, the kids were a little restless for there weren't any gifts for them. Although they had been told they would get them on the sixth of January— that they had better behave or else they would get coal in their stockings, they weren't really convinced about the postponement.

"How about you, Rocky, are you waiting for the sixth for Mary?" Yolanda whispered into his ear.

For a moment, Rocky was confused in that his sister Mary was there. On realizing which Mary, he answered that he had planned to go see her later. And yes, he had something for her.

Towards eight o'clock, Rocky drove to Mary's house where the family was having coffee and pastry. Because he had eaten so much at his home, he politely refused anything at all. Alone with Mary in one corner of the living room, Rocky gave her his Christmas gift, a pin with the image of a boxer on it. Without hesitation, she quickly put it on her lapel, while she puckered her lips for a secret kiss. When he was about to leave, however, she walked him to the car. In the dark, they kissed passionately with Mary telling him she loved him. She then passed her finger over the scar of the left eye. "You know," she said, "I don't like the sport."

"Don't worry; it won't be forever."

The world of boxing had Tony Zale and Rocky Graziano, two other favorite sons, fighting for the world title.

January 13 came around fast, and as fast he put Beau Jack away, thus vindicating the TKO suffered the previous fight. With that victory, Al Flora decided to celebrate 1947 as though the new year had just begun again. Well before midnight, however, Rocky predictively asked to be excused.

The next scheduled fight was an eight rounder for February with Joey Fredda, an up-coming kid from Wilkes Barre, known for his knock out punch. In fact, he had floored several boxers. During the training, Gene Machinist stayed close to Rocky, not only to keep him company but to help him as well. The two made frequent trips to Bunker Hill. On his last run, Gene was waiting to talk with Rocky about the fight.

"I'm so nervous," Rocky confessed to Gene, upon leaving the locker room for the ring

"You're not afraid, are you?" Gene asked, a worried expression on his face.

"I guess I'm always a little scared before I go into the ring. You never know what will happen next. For this one, I know I have to knock him out before he knocks me out. So, I'm going to start right in."

"We're with you, champ. Go get him!" Phil ordered.

With the sound of the bell, Rocky ran to the center of the ring and quickly began with a barrage of punches the likes of which no crowd had seen before. Joey, however, kept on pulling back, thus avoiding the major blows.

At the end of the round, Al Flora walked to the corner to caution Rocky on his tactics, instructing him to preserve his energy, that Joey was not going to go down that easily.

In fact, Joey did not go down. Neither did Rocky, who commanded the fight, winning it unanimously. With that victory, the sports world began to talk about Rocky for nomination for Rookie of the Year.

Still nineteen years old, Rocky fought and won another convincing bout against Chubby Wright. With that, Al Flora and Pete Fulton began negotiation to have Rocky participate in the Championship of the Coal Regions. Rocky was to fight Patsy Gall the evening of March 27 in the Stadium so as to attract a large crowd. The winner of the Gall-Castellani fight would then meet either Joe Falco, Gene Boland or Billy Kilroy. And the winner of the latter would tangle with Sugar Ray Robinson, the undisputed champion of champions according to many experts. When Robinson gave his blessings, Al Flora, Bob Haimes and the other promoters quickly got the ball rolling.

Young Rocky Castellani's Fifth Championship

Rocky read a lot about Patsy Gall in the weeks before the fight. According to the press, Gall didn't stand a chance against Rocky. Yet, Gall had fought some 80 bouts and had met up with some of the best punchers in the world. One reporter, however, talked about Gall being a terrific counter puncher who did his best fighting inside.

Wearing his U.S. Marine Corps robe, he climbed the ring to the enthusiastic cheers of the crowd. Rocky danced around for a few moments, then stopped to look down ringside. There seated in one long row were his father, Yolanda, Anna and Mary with their respective husbands, uncle Mike, Phil, Gene, Red, Father Dolan and several more of his close friends and buddies. After giving a wave with his glove, he began to dance again, looking and acting like a middleweight champion.

Throwing left hooks and right hand smashes to the body, Gall endeavored to weaken Rocky and then apply the crusher— a "Bolo" punch he had used so effectively against such outstanding fighters as Billy Alvarez, Jimmy McDonough, Chavos Ramos and Curly Denton. Young Rocky, remembering what he had heard by experts like Billy Soose, when Gall got close, he used the rabbit punch as an equalizer. The match, as most saw it, was between youth and experience, with most observers predicting in favor of Rocky. He punched his way out of every situation Gall placed him in, often giving back double what he got from Gall. "You want to play rough," young Rocky said to himself in one instance, "then here it goes."

Although the fight went the full eight rounds, Rocky once again won the bout handily. At the moment of the decision, the crowd went into jubilation. Yolanda couldn't help but jump up and down, and next to Rocky himself, perhaps the one that was happier was his father. On his way to the locker, the crowd rushed around him, making it difficult for him to move ahead. Seeing himself surrounded as he was, he didn't make much of an effort to move forward, for he loved the attention.

Inebriated by that sweet victory, Rocky headed home where family and friends were waiting. Before going to bed, he noticed his father walking around the house bragging about his young son Attilio becoming the middleweight champ of the Coal Regions, considered during this time the boxing capital of the world. Uncle Mike and his clan bragged about the fact that Rocky now ranked fifth. Happy over the attention, he nevertheless withdrew to his room. Laying flat on his back, he remembered his mother, wishing she had been there to share in the celebration. Then, just as he was about to close his eyes, he wondered where or how it was all going to end. Mary Jugus was on his mind, and he knew she didn't like what he was doing.

Pete Fulton and Al Flora did not waste time in lining up Jiggs Donohue for a May 12th eight rounder at Scranton's Wattras Armory. With Rocky winning the bout, by knocking Jiggs through the ropes in the seventh, Mike Barrett, a promoter, signed Rocky to fight a return match with Billy Kilroy. Flora and Fulton agreed to use the ball park stadium in Dunmore, Pennsylvania, and the match was scheduled for the middle of June. Unfortunately, Mike Barrett begged off the Kilroy Castellani fight, getting Gene Boland in Kilroy's place.

While all the successful fighting was taking place, Rocky continued on his quest in a quiet but obsessive way, paying attention only to boxing and to no one else. Mary Jugus, although she loved him, began to complain to her mother.

"I never see him," she said. I saw him once when he got his new car and that's it."

"Of course, he's always in the ring. He doesn't have time for anything else. But, be patient. This can't go on forever."

"It seems like forever to me," said Mary.

"Don't worry. At this pace, something will happen and he will be out of it before you know it."

"Mother, what are you saying?" she asked in a tone of anger.

"I'm saying only what I've seen with so many others in that sport. Soon or later, something happens. But don't worry, either way, Rocky will make a wonderful husband."

"Husband! We're not even engaged," said Mary.

"I know. But he'll come around soon," Mrs. Jugus commented, sure of herself. Above all, she was sure about Rocky's ability to make it with or without boxing. "But tell me Mary, have you spent time with his family?"

"Not really. But you know, he talks a lot about his mother. He misses her a great deal."

"Look at us. Your father died and we haven't been the same since. But, one thing is to be without a father; another is to be without a mother. We mothers do make the difference. No matter how old the children are when a mother dies or leaves, the children always suffer. The fact that Rocky talks about his mother is good proof," said Mrs. Jugus.

"I guess so. Sometimes he also talks about his two sisters that got married before they finished high school. Rocky thinks that if his mother had been alive they would not have gotten married so soon. Mind you, he's not complaining."

"I understand. In any case, remember what we've been saying because you too will be married one day.

Tommy Ryan and Rocky

And once you have children, your first responsibility will be to them," Mrs. Jugus said in a serious tone, thinking how strange life is. "Look at our two families: we're without a father, and they without a mother. You know what worries me? No one knows what can happen next," Mrs. Jugus continued.

On May 28, just as he was about to leave home for his early run, Anne arrived unexpectedly. She had come to wish him a happy birthday and to ask him what he wanted for a present. Rocky answered that for as long as he had his boxing gloves pin, he was happy. After telling her to wait for Yolanda to get up, he hugged her and walked out to begin his run.

Gene Boland was well known for his *in fighting*. Worried, Flora got Oscar Boyd, a tough middleweight who had fought with Holman Williams and Tony Zale, the middleweight champion of the world, to teach Rocky the techniques of in fighting. The bout was scheduled for June 10. Meanwhile, Boland sent a letter to the press, saying he was going to win over the "cocky young kid from Luzerne" with a knock out, even if Rocky was the former Marine Champ and the new Champion of the Coal Regions.

Finally 20 years old and with five championships under his belt, Rocky had no trouble putting Gene Boland away. After the fight, Gene said that Rocky was "one of the nicest boxers and cleanest fighter he ever met."

Castellani's fame was spreading so rapidly that promoters everywhere were trying to schedule their fighters against him. Matchmakers Frank Shepard and Irving Cohen, who managed Rocky Graziano, got in touch with Flora and Fulton and arranged a July 2nd bout with Ernie Butler at the West Side Armory.

Rocky fought a rather even fight up to the sixth. Ernie held his own; at times, it seemed he even had the upper hand. Then in the seventh, Rocky opened with powerful lefts that kept Butler off balance.

Toward the end of the round, Rocky landed a hard right sending Butler reeling along the ropes. In the eighth, Rocky continued with a barrage of punches, bringing the crowd to its feet. When the bell sounded, Butler was completely without strength and barely standing up.

In an interview, Mike Capriano (Ernie Butler's trainer and handler who had been sure that Ernie would have beaten Rocky) said that "Castellani had improved 1000% since his last fight."

But the bout everyone was waiting for was finally scheduled. Now that Billy Kilroy was ready, Flora and Fulton arranged it for September 19 in Scranton's Wattras Armory. With Barrett promoting the bout, wheels were put in motion to make the bout a historical one. Knowing how important it was to beat Kilroy, Rocky continued to train as though his life depended on that victory. Meanwhile, offers from other promoters kept on pouring in from many sections of the country, especially from New York. And as usual, experts and sports writers took sides. Billy Stevens, boxing expert, picked Kilroy; most others picked the marine from the coal region.

With the Armory packed to the hilt and the fans chanting the name of the marine, Rocky began the eight rounder in a slow and deliberate pace, jabbing with his left, hitting with his right uppercuts. As he was winning practically every round, he continued till the end, winning the fight convincingly.

Tommy Ryan and Madison Square Garden

Ringside was Tommy Ryan, a promoter. Convinced about Rocky's potentials, Mr. Ryan spoke to Flora to entice him to bring Rocky to New York. When Fulton and Rocky learned of live television coverage, they all agreed to the move, signing a contract for an eight round bout with Lenny *Boom Boom* Mancini in Madison Square Garden. To train for the fight, Mr. Ryan arranged for Rocky to stay at a camp in Long

Pond, New Jersey.

On the evening of September 19, with Tony Pallone and Tony Janiro featured for the main bout, Rocky outdid himself by scoring a clean and convincing victory over the feared scrapper, Mancini. When young Rocky left the ring, the crowd gave him a resounding applause. Certainly, Rocky had now become another favorite son of the New York fans as well. Even when in the showers, promoters approached him for upcoming matches.

Al Flora, Peter Fulton and Tommy Ryan immediately scheduled Rocky for his first main event fight to be held at the Saint Nick's Arena— a Madison Garden affiliate— with Tony Riccio, the well known contender. Well along in their training for the bout, Riccio took sick and withdrew, thus canceling the bout.

Fighting for the Underprivileged Children Fund

With the New York bout canceled, Rocky accepted to fight in behalf of the Kiwanis Club, which would receive a percentage of the proceeds to aid crippled and underprivileged children. His managers signed up Vic Costa, a fighter who had been around, with fights against Boland, Tony Pallone, Phil Palmer and Billy Graham, the future uncrowned world welterweight champion. Vic had the reputation of a spoiler in that he enjoyed stopping upcoming young boxers like Rocky. Only 20 years old, Rocky became the subject of many sports writers in conjunction with Vic Costa's record against young fighters. When the fight was over, no one speculated any longer. Once again, keeping Costa off his feet with tremendous and relentless barrages of left and right shots to the face and head, Rocky dropped the veteran boxer to the canvas— a physical wreck during the third round. The fans were wild-eyed at Rocky's dazzling exhibition of speed and accurate punching.

With the results fairly well covered in the national

press, Castellani once again got all kinds of offers, resulting in his managers making promises they could not keep. Ryan signed Tony Riccio for a Madison Square Garden bout while Flora wanted the bout to be held in Wilkes-Barre. Furthermore, the press was insinuating that the real beneficiaries of the Castellani-Costa fight were Rocky's managers. On top of that, some of the press criticized the managers for getting second rate opponents for Rocky, insinuating that until now Rocky hadn't really been challenged.

Matchmaker Lou Boch offered Ryan 30% of the gate for Rocky to fight Jimmy King, saying that Castellani would be no match for King. Instead, Ryan signed up for a main with Tony Riccio. On learning about this, Lou got angry. "We promoters," he said, "have a right to ask Rocky to fight opponents who will attract crowds large enough to assure a profit. We are not in business for love either, and the fans must get a decent break too, from the fighters they support as whole-heartedly as they have supported Rocky... Every fighter with a reputation wants the Fort Knox Gold and an opponent he can blow over with his breath. I regret to say that the managers of Rocky Castellani had become listed in that class too."

While people like Lou Boch were speaking aloud about things they didn't think were right, Mr. Castellani proudly made the rounds with his ever increasing number of Italian-speaking friends who had become his son's vociferous fans. In learning about even the slightest derogatory comment about Rocky, they immediately defended him. Mr. Castellani Sr., of course, prided in the turn of events. He even began to dress better. Even Yolanda dressed better. More importantly, for the past several months there was more food in the house.

Weighing 154 pounds, Rocky was in the best physical shape. In his main event with Tony Riccio on November 10 at St. Nick's, Rocky maintained a steady pace throughout his first Main-go ten rounder. Referee

Jack Appel scored it 5-3-2, Judge Arthur Susskind 7-3, and Judge Nick B. Gamboli 8-2: Castellani.

While Rocky was winning his matches, his promoters were arguing over locations for the matches. Tommy stressed New York; Al Flora stressed Pennsylvania. Tommy sought better and different names; Al wanted Tony Janiro. The two finally agreed to have the next match in Wilkes Barre, a ten round re-match bout on December 19 with Lenny *Boom Boom* Mancini.

While training *blindly* for the bout (for Rocky nothing else really existed— not even Mary, it seemed), he learned he had been named Wyoming Valley Athlete of the Year. That evening, he made an exception to his training schedule to go visit Mary at her house.

While sitting in the living room, Mary complained a little bit about the fact that he didn't go to her house as often as she had hoped for.

"Be patient," he answered. "The time will come when you'll see too much of me."

When he left, around ten o'clock, Mrs. Jugus made it a point to speak with her daughter. "I know you are disappointed about his not coming over as often. But be patient..."

"But Mom, all he lives for is boxing! I don't even know his sisters, and they're my age."

"And I know you don't like it. Neither do I. It's so, so..."

"So brutal..." said Mary.

"And so...," Mrs. Jugus repeated, grasping for a word she did not know. She wanted to say that Rocky was on a one dimensional track which was both good and bad, but that she wasn't sure what was good or bad. She only knew that Rocky was good for her daughter. "Do you love him?" she asked.

"I love him, but at times I wonder if there's any future for us," said Mary.

Two Deserved Awards

Now that Rocky had been named Athlete of the Year, he drew a full house for the rematch with Mancini. As expected by the many fans, Rocky fought such a great fight that he was given the credit for permanently *retiring* Mancini from the ring. (The name of *Boom Boom,* however, would be taken up by Mr. Mancini's son, who became a world champion boxer in the 1980s).

Finishing the year undefeated, champions like Rocky Graziano, Jake LaMotta, Sugar Ray Robinson, Tony Zale and others all watched the record that *young* Rocky was piling up, each knowing that sooner or later one of them would wind up fighting him.

In one of the great upsets in the history of boxing, Sugar Ray Robinson, the five time middleweight champion of the world, lost to Randolph Turpin of England. This turn of events indirectly affected Attilio Castellani, Jr.

Ring Magazine had Castellani and Turpin as the top contenders for the Rookie of the Year Award. Turpin, youngest of three fighting brothers, ran off a remarkable record for his first year in professional boxing. Because he was only 19 years old, he was able to fight only six rounders in England. This situation worked in favor of Rocky. In 1948, *Ring Magazine* gave its last award to Rocky Castellani. Rocky Marciano, the future undefeated World Heavyweight Champion, was also a rookie, but lost out. The award caused a veritable pandemonium of joy and festivities throughout Luzerne, but especially at the home of Mr. Castellani, who had gathered many of his relatives and friends for the celebration. Conspicuous in the group were uncle Mike and Father Dolan.

A fan

Chapter 13

Rocky's Management

Rocky's three managers all had other interests besides boxing. Pete Fulton had his produce business, Al Flora had his gym complex, and Tommy Ryan had things going in New York that few people could figure out. There was already talk about Tommy being connected with the underworld. Aside from these diverse interests, each had a different philosophy and different approach on managing Rocky, and each pulled in his own direction. Rocky, who was still only a young man, never really understood his role and relationship with them. Neither was he strong enough to go on his own or look for others to help him. All he saw was fighting— how to become a better boxer, and eventually a champion. Managing and promoting were not his bag. Because he was such a good boxer, he drew packed houses all the time, which meant money, with the promoters fighting for their shares.

For Rocky, the winter snows and brutal winds were not as overpowering anymore. His house was warm and there was plenty of food. He traveled in a new car which had all the options. He had achieved in civilian life what he had gotten in the marines; for this, he was thankfully contented.

Meanwhile, Al Flora worked with Mr. Dewey, the

matchmaker of the new Wilkes Barre Athletic Club, and arranged a bout with Jimmy King for January 15. Tommy Ryan arranged to have Tony Pallone spar with Rocky. With Dewey in the picture, Rocky's managers and promoters also got Frankie Cardanelli and Joe Rodona to help with the training. They all feared King's power and agility, especially his left; because of that, they got Jimmy Smith to help. They were also a bit preoccupied with a cut over Rocky's right eye and feared King might use it as a lever.

There was a huge snow storm during the night of the fight, and it was miserably cold. Although Rocky did not like the cold, he was heartened to see the more than 5,000 fans cheering and chanting his name.

With the sound of the bell, Rocky ran to the center of the ring in a style the fight fans had never witnessed before. He immediately started with his left jabs and swinging rights to King's jaws. King, however, bounced back. Aware of the softness over Rocky's right eye, and with the help of his assistants who knew the same thing, began to aim for that spot, succeeding in opening the cut four times. Feeling in trouble, Rocky knew he had to stay away from King. As important, he had to over box so as to maintain the lead in the points he had gained. Toward the end of the fight, King tried to floor Rocky with wild rights; Rocky, likewise, swung wildly, missing practically all, fighting and slugging instead of using his usual skillful boxing procedure. With many of his female admirers yelling to him to take his time, Rocky succeeded in avoiding King's feared left hook. Worried over Rocky's bleeding eye, Johnny Kelly, the referee, called the doctor in. By this round, Rocky was ahead in points and knew it. When the doctor approached him, Rocky had an apparent anxious expression.

"You've got let me go on," he said, almost out of breath.

"Let's take a look," the doctor answered, his voice almost drowned by the cheering fans. "It doesn't look too good, Rocky," he said. How do you feel? Do you think you can go on another round?"

"Sure Doc, sure I can."

With the doctor's permission, the crowd roared with pleasure.

Knowing the fight was in doubt, Rocky succeeded in keeping King away from the eye. He finished the last round, but knew he hadn't done very well. As he waited for the judges and referee to announce the result, Rocky said a prayer.

It was answered when the announcement was made he had won by decision, to the tumultuous joy of his fans.

Before the crowd was dismissed, Frank Sheppard, former matchmaker for the Fight Club, went to the microphone to auction off Rocky's gloves on behalf of the Infantile Paralysis Fund, and got a total of 150 dollars. Mr. Flora bid on them.

Injuries

At the Wilkes-Barre Homeopathic Hospital, Dr. Casterline closed Rocky's laceration with five stitches. "You know," Rocky said, "the eye bothered me from the fourth round on."

With doctor's orders to stay away from boxing for several weeks, Rocky was released the next morning. Instead of going to the gym, this time he went directly home to rest.

His popularity so immense, Rocky received several proposition from female admirers. "Look, it's good to go out with other girls," Al Flora commented. "After all, you're only twenty. You don't want to get stuck with one girl, do you? Listen to me, go out and have a good time."

While the scar over his eye seemed to be healing well, Rocky began to complain about a consistent pain in his badly bruised hip. When Flora, Ryan and Fulton learned from Dr. Pumma it would take four months for the hip injury to heal, they quickly scrapped a March bout with a boxer by the name of Green and scheduled a bout with Leo Sawicki for May 13 in Wilkes-Barre instead. Henceforth, Dr. Pumma would be present at Rocky's fights.

With Rocky feeling better physically, Tommy insisted on having him train for the Sawicki fight at Stillman's Gym in New York City. Here, Rocky learned a new punch which he nicknamed *Zolar*. With Frankie helping him, Rocky regained the physical fitness he had enjoyed in the past. He especially liked his *Zolar* punch which he now threw directly from the shoulder with the result that when he tagged, the opponent certainly felt its power.

Sawicki, a well known Boston Brawler who had never been kayoed, had the press wondering about Rocky. The reporters knew about Rocky's eye trouble. Now that they also knew about the bruised hip and how long it took to heal, they wondered about Rocky's future.

"Don't you worry," reiterated Ryan. "When you finish with Sawicki, you'll be in line for other great fights. Just get in there and do the best job you can."

"Ya," Rocky commented blandly, knowing that guys like Rudy Campo, Johnny Green, Jay Paganelli and Tony Falco— all kayo artists— had not been able to floor Sawicki. Besides, Sawicki, the iron-chinned challenger, had just won a very convincing bout against Jess *Bulldog* Baker.

The night of the fight, the Wilkes-Barre facility was packed. In addition to the usual fans, many of whom had become fanatics by now, there were also many young kids. These, wearing jackets with the name of *Rocky* emblazoned across the back, comprised a veritable cheering section. These young people had grown fond of Rocky, seeing him as their friend. They liked his modesty and appreciated the things he did for charitable organizations and for the underprivileged young ones. Certainly, because he was the champion of their region, they placed him on a pedestal.

The kids were in for a good treat— such is the case when the favorite wins, especially when the victory is good.

In the fourth round, Rocky unleashed one of his zolar punches to Sawicki's solar plexus for a KO. When referee completed the count, the crowd cheered ecstatically.

With the excuse of May 28 being Rocky's birthday— his 21st, not his 22nd— Tommy Ryan scheduled a bout with Harold Green in New York's Madison Square Garden.

With Ryan getting his way, he insured to have Rocky once again train in Stillman's Gym. When he learned that Rocky's name appeared on the Garden's marquis, Tommy took Rocky for a ride. On approaching the Garden, he slowed down, coming to a stop just before the marquis.

"How do you like it?" Ryan asked, pointing to Rocky's name above that of former champions Joe Louis and Joe Walcott.

Needless to say, Rocky was overwhelmed. When he had traveled to the Pacific by way of California, he fantasized about Hollywood movie stars. Now, before his eyes, his real dream had come true. Seeing how happy Rocky was, Ryan arranged for a photographer to take Rocky's picture in front of the huge marquis.

While Rocky trained under the watchful eye of Tommy, Al Flora was making other arrangements for Rocky, who, because he was so young and full of energy, did not realize he might be fighting too many consecutive bouts.

Jim Jennings, sports writer for the *New York Daily Mirror,* described the looming melee as a "slugfest", reminding the fans that Green had been in the ring with world champions like Marcel Cerdan, and that he had won two times against Rocky Graziano in 1944. To get back in the lime light, Green badly needed this televised victory over Rocky Castellani.

The "slugfest" began as predicted. Green floored

Rocky in the second with a thunderous blow to the head, forcing Rocky to take a full count. Wobbling, he managed to finish the round without further damage even though Green pressed to extremes. In the sixth, Rocky caught Green with a right hand for a count of nine, getting up just as the bell sounded. With the tenth round drawing to a close, Rocky wasn't sure just what his birthday bout was going to bring about. The Associated Press scored four each with two even; Judge Jack O'Sullivan scored it 5-4-1 Green; Judge Charlie Shortell scored it 5-4-1 Castellani; Referee Eddie Joseph scored it 7-3 Castellani. With that victory, as close as it was, Rocky's entourage went crazy with excitement.

The next morning, Rocky became the toast of New York and of the nation, with his story and pictures appearing in practically every newspaper. *Ringside Reporter* had Rocky's birthday and fight results plastered all over its pages.

In *Boxing* Magazine, Billy Stevens of the National Boxing Association, rated Tony Zale, the Middleweight Champion, with Marcel Cerdan and Bert Lytell as contenders, Honorable mention to Rocky Castellani.

After a July fight with another Italian boxer from the Bronx— the tough Mickey Zanagra, which Rocky won but not without another severe cut over his eye, Tommy Ryan began to talk about a future match with the Middleweight Champion of the World.

Everyone continued to want a shot at Rocky, to be the first to beat him by a KO. Henry Cohen, manager of Henry Lee was convinced his boxer could defeat Rocky: "If I've got to put money on the line to guarantee the scrap, I'll do it. Just tell me where the check is to be sent." But Rocky's managers had already signed to fight Herby Kronowitz.

Meanwhile, Rocky took some time out to help with a benefit for the Wyoming Valley Community Chest. With Rocky the official judge, he presided over the event to choose the official mascot title. On being given what he thought were seven unusual All American boys, Rocky decided to make them all mascots, presenting a permanent statuette of the mythical Red Feather Kid to Bob, Fred, Charlie, Phil, Andy, George and Paul.

Al Flora Bows Out

A few days before the fight, Al Flora and Attorney Lowery asked Rocky to help with a boxing program for about 200 kids at an all day outing held at Pocono Lake by the Addonizio family. Assisted by Al Flora, Rocky refereed in all the bouts. Among the outstanding participants were Michael (Gabe) Flloyd, former Golden Glove Champ. But the biggest champ of all was Rocky. The kids hung close to him like glue, all asking him questions about boxing and especially about the upcoming fights. Uppermost in their minds: when would he become a world champion?

"When God wills it," answered one of the ten priest assisting in the program.

God willed that Rocky should win the bout with Kronowitz by taking nine of ten rounds. By the end of the fight, Kronowitz was a bloody mess. Except for a cut over his left eye, which began to give him more than just annoyance, Rocky seemed in good shape. Both he and his managers ignored the cut as inconsequential though it bled a little more than it should have.

Pursuant to that fight, in an edition of *Sports Week,* Jack Dempsey rated Rocky Castellani ahead of Rocky Graziano.

While taking a pause from his training, he heard a radio announcement that the great Babe Ruth had died. Rocky thought about Babe Ruth and wished he could have seen him play. He also wished he could have been present to view the body inside the main entrance to Yankee Stadium along side the more than two hundred thousand fans.

As Rocky piled up one success after another, his managers continued to squabble over Rocky's future. Ryan continued to insist on making New York the permanent headquarters of Rocky. Meanwhile, on October 8, he knocked out Walter Cartier in the seventh round. On November 18, he defeated Sonny Horne in ten rounds. After each of his wins, Rocky was deluged with congratulatory telegrams.

Impressed by Rocky's string of victories, Sol Strauss, the producer of the Horne fight, talked about a match between Rocky and Jake LaMotta, the notorious *Bronx Bull*. Tommy Ryan had other plans, however. He wanted Rocky to meet Robert Villemain, the French Welterweight, or Charley Fusari, or Tony Janiro or Marcel Cerdan— but not LaMotta. Neither was right, for, Rocky's next fight was going to be with Al Priest.

Though Al Flora had given up his financial interest in Rocky, he continued to be on the best of terms with the young boxer. Afterall, Flora had become like a father to him, helping him with everything, from buying clothes, to counseling him spiritually and financially. In the rift between Tommy and Al, Rocky kept neutral, knowing only that he had to continue with his career as a professional boxer. Even though Tommy won, Al continued to help Rocky in his personal affairs.

When Rocky's stepmother got ill and landed in the hospital, Al accompanied Rocky to visit her. At the hospital, the women patients were impressed to see the famous Rocky visit his stepmother, especially on the day in which he had to fight.

"I'm going to win my fight; you've got to win yours," he told a lady friend of his stepmother. When he returned to the hospital a few days later, Rocky approached the same lady. "I won my fight; you gotta win yours," causing the woman to regain her composure and to begin to eat.

Aside from his visit to the hospital and spending

time with his father and sister, Rocky finally decided to spend some more time with Mary. The two went out several times. It became clear to Mary that he was really serious about her. She now began to like the attention he was giving her. She also liked the gifts he kept on buying her.

In seeing her daughter so happy, Mrs. Jugus predicted it would not be long before her daughter would be getting married.

The split between Al Flora and Tommy Ryan had not been made public. When it finally surfaced, it hit like a bombshell. Rocky's fans did not like it at all, especially those from the coal region. Young Rocky was their idol and felt that by going with Ryan, they would lose him.

In an interview, Flora expressed nothing but the highest praise for Rocky, saying that Rocky, because he was such a serious young man, was as good as Graziano, LaMotta and Zale, that Rocky could have been a great athlete in any sport.

Sports reporter Mike Bernstein was speechless when he heard that Rocky had opted to go with Ryan. Rocky tried to smooth over the situation by saying there had been a business misunderstanding between Al and Tommy, that things would be squared away. Bernstein, however, predicted that with Rocky leaving Flora, Rocky's popularity would drop a thousandfold. Furthermore, the press began to report on rumors that Tommy had other deals going on.

To keep his fans happy, Ryan arranged to have Rocky fight Al Priest in Scranton. Scheduled as the first fight of 1949, Rocky's fans piled in the familiar Wattras Armory. This time, besides Mr. Castellani, just about every friend of Rocky was present, including Father Dolan, Phil, Gene and the rest of the Rose Hill gang. As expected, they were in for a treat and got just what they wanted— a rather convincing victory. Rocky, however, although he did not show it, began to feel the weight of those punches on his eyes. Once again, he bled from a cut.

Allowing Rocky to spend only the day after the fight with his family, Ryan took Rocky to New York to sign for a bout with Charley Fusari to be held in New York City— *The Big Apple!*

In signing the contract, Rocky felt a bit uneasy. Something was wrong but he couldn't identify the cause.

"What's the matter, Rocky?" Fusari asked, a smirk on his face. "Are you having second thoughts?"

Surprised by that tone, Rocky looked straight into Fusari's eyes, in a way he had never done before with any other fighter. "I'll see you on the canvas," Rocky said in a serious tone.

"We'll see," Fusari retorted with a derisive laugh.

Scheduled for Friday night, and going for his 20th victory in a row, he would be on live national television again from Madison Square Garden, New York City. Tommy expected the bout to be a slug fest, knowing how extremely important Rocky's victory would be for his career. Afterall, he had great plans for his young boxer.

Two Big Losses

The evening of February 18 proved to be a jolt for Rocky as much as for Ryan and for the thousands of fans all over the country. Rocky was not himself. Outwardly, he looked the same as he always did; inside, he felt scared for the first time in his life. To compensate for this, at the sound of the bell, Rocky went out to the center of the ring like a wild man, throwing everything in the book. Fusari, who had been around too long to play the sucker role, let Rocky punch himself out, acting as though he was ready to drop to the canvas any moment. Every time Rocky tried to drop Fusari, Fusari seemed to manage to strike back. Toward the latter rounds, Fusari's punches began to hit their mark more and more. In the eight, Fusari dropped his right to the head and jaw of Rocky. When it was over, Rocky lost the ten

Mary

rounder.

Reflecting on that fight, Rocky recognized he had lost it in the first round. "I was scared," he admitted. "I didn't have my usual confidence. I came running, rushing out like a chimpanzee. I went wild and threw everything I had. I left my fight in the first round."

The fight was a set back. Tommy immediately tried a remedy by scheduling a bout with Tony DeMicco, which Rocky won without difficulties, and another with the feared Tony Janiro. In the latter, scheduled in Scranton, Rocky was in tip top form, beating the undefeated Janiro silly with a lopsided victory.

Living in New Jersey with the Ryans proved difficult for Rocky. He missed his family very much; now, he missed Mary more than ever. Something different was happening to him; he was not thinking solely of boxing. The more he fought and saw how so many of his opponents were ending in *pulp,* he began to make comparisons between himself and them. He even daydreamed. And in these thoughts, the image of Mary appeared on a regular basis. Her face was clear; those of his boxing opponents full of bruises and cuts. He passed his hand over his face, his finger stopping over the cut on his left eye. "Do I want to end up looking like them?" he asked as he looked into the mirror, pleased that in spite of the many bouts, he still looked very decent.

Having won over Janiro, Rocky stopped by a Jewelry store and bought an engagement ring. When he told Tommy what he had done and that he planned to go back home to give Mary the ring, Tommy got angry. He felt, like most managers, that getting married or even engaged at that time would have ruined Castellani's career as a fighter.

"Hang on," Tommy suggested in an obvious calm voice. "You've got all kinds of time. You're only 22. Besides, I got you scheduled for a bout with Tony Riccio."

The bout proved another failure for Rocky in that

he fought to a draw. Feeling somewhat humiliated, he went out and bought himself a new yellow convertible.

"Look," he said to Tommy, "I've gotta start thinking about other things. I'm leaving for a few days for Luzerne. I decided to give Mary the ring after all."

Mary's Engagement

After supper, with Mrs. Jugus doing the dishes, Rocky finally had a chance to be alone with Mary. After he said he loved her, he asked her how she felt. Without saying a word, she put her hands around his neck and kissed him. "Of course I love you. I've always loved you," she repeated emphatically.

"In that case, will you marry me?"

"What did you say?"

"I'm asking you to marry me."

"What about your boxing?"

"I'm sick and tired of living in New Jersey. Besides, I think we should get married and start a family of our own. What do you say?"

"I love you and I want to marry you."

That was what he wanted to hear. He pulled out the box and opened it. "This is for you. I hope you like it."

Ecstatic, Mary put it on her finger and immediately rushed to the kitchen to show her mother. In the meantime, the telephone rang. Mary went to answer it.

"It's Tommy. He wants to speak with you."

"We got Kid Gavilan!" Tommy boasted. When Rocky remained silent, Tommy continued, "Well, what do you say? Is it or is not a fight?"

"It's a fight!" he answered unconvincingly, and hung up.

When news broke out, fans, reporters, and promoters alike quickly began to make their predictions. Some insisted that Rocky would win by a knockout; others, more conservative and knowledgeable, wondered if a bout with the famous Gavilan was not premature for Rocky. Even Flora got into the act, saying that Rocky should not have accepted.

The money for that fight was one of the biggest purses in Rocky's career. What, in Madison Square Garden and on national television, Rocky and Tommy scored rather well financially. For Rocky, however, it was not going to be so great!

The Cuban took the bout by beating Rocky rather soundly. All of a sudden, 1949 was not a good year. It was only September and he had one draw and two losses. With this realization, Rocky began to think more and more about his family and about Mary. Tommy, realizing Rocky needed some time for soul searching, told Rocky to go spend a few days back home.

In Luzerne, Rocky found more time to go visit his friends and relatives. In spite of the recent loss, wherever he went he was received like a hero. At times, his fans were so boisterous as to embarrass him.

"Look, I just lost to Gavilan," he said to his uncle Mike.

"Sure, but we know you'll come back," he answered. "Name me one boxer who has ended his career without a defeat."

Rocky thought it over. When he didn't come up with an answer, his uncle encouraged him not to be discouraged.

He got the same treatment from Mrs. Jugus, who, although she secretely prayed that Rocky would stop boxing altogether, nevertheless encouraged him to go on to win. Mary, on the other hand, made no bones about wanting Rocky to stop fighting. Yolanda just told her brother that she wanted only what he wanted. And Mr. Castellani, as proud as ever, even in fragile health, sided with his famous son.

Win he did for the rest of 1949, with two return bouts, one against Tony Riccio and the other against Harold Green, with Rocky winning as though he had never suffered a loss in his life.

Broken Hand

With General MacArthur landing in Korea in 1950, for the next three years America would be fighting what turned out to be the first of a series of unpopular wars or skirmishes. When news broke, Rocky wondered if he would be recalled.

In his January 27th first fight of the year against Ernie Durando, Rocky was to receive his first real set back. In the fourth round, Rocky began to slug away, going for an early knockout. On connecting with a thunderous right to Durando's head, Rocky suddenly felt an excruciating pain in his right hand. Between rounds, Rocky said nothing about the pain. At the bell, he ran to the center of the ring to assume fighting. For some reason, the hand did not hurt as much. As a result, he continued to box, but mainly slapping with his hand. When the referee noticed Rocky was not putting it together, he told Rocky to stop slapping. By the end of the bout, Rocky could barely slap his right hand around. He finished the bout, winning by a decision. When Frankie took off the glove, he noticed Rocky's broken hand.

With Al Flora out of the picture, Tommy got a stronghold on young Castellani. He arranged and scheduled the fights; he also controlled Rocky's private life. Uppermost in his mind, however, was the middleweight title. In his attempt to achieve that goal, Tommy often overstepped his limits.

During a social get together at the home of Tommy, while Mrs. Ryan was serving sandwiches, Mary wondered aloud about Rocky's immediate future, now that he was not fighting as much. She was interested in learning how much free time Rocky was going to devote to her.

"Not much time, Mary," Tommy answered— a deliberate worried expression on his face. "We're getting ready for the title, and Rocky has to maintain a stricter regimen, especially now that he's recovering from the broken hand."

"Where's that leave us? We're engaged, you know!" she stated in a harsh voice, causing Rocky to look up.

"I don't know what to tell you," Tommy answered shrugging his shoulders and looking at Rocky's hand in the sling.

"What about you Rocky! What do have to say about this?" she asked in an angry tone.

On seeing the tension, Mrs. Ryan, who hardly ever entered into conversations when her husband was present, intervened. "Won't you have a sandwich?" she asked Mary, who accepted gracefully.

When Rocky emphasized the need to train for a shot at the title, implying that he would have to spend a lot of time at the Ryans, Mary exploded. She took the ring and threw it at Rocky, saying that the engagement was off. Embarrassed because he had never seen Mary so angry nor known that side of her character, Rocky picked up the ring.

"Alright, we'll talk about it later. Meanwhile, just relax. I don't want you to worry," Rocky said, reassuring her.

Tommy, standing up next to his wife, after hesitating a few moments, looked at the young woman. "Mary," he said condescendingly, "all I'm trying to do is save Rocky's career."

"And I'm trying to save Rocky," she retorted angrily.

Feeling the tension, and to keep it from getting worse, Mrs. Ryan asked her husband to help her in the kitchen. Alone, Rocky promised Mary that things would work out, that he would go see her every weekend. "If you want to, we can even get married— right now, if you wish."

Surprised by Rocky's seriousness, Mary realized she had overreacted. She took back the ring and kissed him tenderly. When Tommy returned and Rocky told him he and Mary were going to get married, Tommy became worried, knowing how many times before love had gotten in the way. Not wanting to make matters worse, he decided not to comment on Rocky's wish.

Semi Secret Marriage

Because Tommy had not been able to schedule any bouts for six months, Rocky found himself with more free time, spending a lot of it with his fiance, especially weekends.

Mrs. Jugus was extremely happy to see Rocky so many times at her house. Like Mary, she was even happier not to see Rocky fighting. Because of the apparent change in Rocky's life style, Mrs. Jugus confided with Mary.

"What's going on between you and Rocky? I get the impression you two are up to something. He's always around here. Mind you, I am very happy to have him here."

"I'm happy too. Mom, he asked me to marry him."

"I know that," Mrs. Jugus quickly answered, a smile on her face.

"We don't mean a regular marriage."

"You're not pregnant, I hope," Mrs. Jugus said, a serious expression on her face.

"No, Mom, nothing like that. You don't have to worry."

With that, Mrs. Jugus gave an evident sigh of relief. "So, what does this all mean?"

Mary explained that Rocky was willing to marry her but to keep it secret until he won the title.

"How do you feel about that," Mrs. Jugus asked.

"I don't know. I have to think about it," said Mary.

All medical reports indicated Rocky's hand healing well. Nevertheless, Tommy wanted to be sure the hand was fine before letting him resume a full training schedule. Because of this concern, Tommy arranged to make a trip to Florida to see this famous specialist he knew.

On their way down, knowing the title was on the line, the two hardly spoke. Both were worried over the broken hand.

After spending the night in a local motel room, the two went to see the doctor. He looked at the hand, then had the nurse prepare Rocky for x-rays. After all the tests were completed, the Doctor asked Rocky how it felt.

"Good! It feels OK," he answered a worried expression on his face, wrinkles on his large forehead.

"There's nothing wrong with your hand. I'd say you've healed well, as though you never had a break. You can resume your career as though this thing never happened."

With that, the three looked at each other, then burst out in laughter, that aura of happiness lasting all the way back in the drive to Pennsylvania.

Meanwhile, the press was giving all kinds of coverage on the goings on with Rocky. On several occasions, they also talked about Tommy Ryan as the "mystery" man behind the young boxer, referring to Tommy as the "New York City Slicker".

"You see," said Mary, "I never liked that man. There's something about him."

With his father, uncle, sister and many friends, including Father Dolan, at ringside, Rocky stood in the ring against Phil Burton. Expectedly, the crowd was anxious, but not as much as Rocky. Luckily, he took charge from the very beginning. Rocky, afterall, had trained well and was in top physical shape. As a result, he handled Burton without many difficulties, to the excitement of his home crowd which was convinced of their hero's complete comeback.

Rocky, however, was not convinced about his hand; and because he did not want to take any chances, he and Tommy decided to call it quits for 1950. That decision caused many people to draw diverse conclusions, some of which was not entirely flattering to the young fighter.

Church Wedding

Holding hands, Rocky and Mary walked into the

sacristy of St. John's Catholic Church, looking for Father Dolan.

"Father," Rocky said, "Mary and I want to be married in the church. Can you help us?"

That was all the priest needed to hear. With the date fixed for the end of the year, the three agreed to have it a private affair; for, otherwise, there would have been difficulties.

Mary and Rocky were successful in keeping their plans secret. On the day of the wedding, they simply went to the church where they got married without any fanfare. After a simple Italian dinner prepared by Connie and Yolanda, the couple left for their honeymoon in the Poconos.

"At one moment during the ceremony, you seemed far away with your thoughts. What were you thinking about?" she said, as she looked at Rocky, who was driving their yellow convertible.

"My mother. I just wished she had been there. I miss her a great deal. I guess I always will."

Coincidentally, as the newly weds were traveling, the radio announced that Jack Dempsey had been presented with the award as the Best Boxer in the first half of the 20th century.

"You know," he commented, "I wish someday to be like him."

Chapter 14

Middleweight Aspirations

For the next two years, Rocky fought a total of 16 bouts. Except for one loss by TKO with Ernie Durando and one draw with Billy Graham, he won them all— three of them by knockouts. His opponents were practically all veterans, and included Bobby Lloyd, Tommy Varsos, Joe DiMartino, Gene Hairston, Joe Giardello, Terry Moore, Ernie Durando, Ralph Jones, Ralph Zanelli, Johnny Bratton, Johnny Lombardo, Jimmy Herring, Vic Cardell and Jimmy Flood. By the end of 1952, there was no doubt as to who the top contender for the middleweight crown was. Even champs like Rocky Graziano and Jack LaMotta, who sat at ringside for many of Rocky's bouts, commented on the fact that Rocky Castellani was the one to watch and to beat. What was even more startling was that Rocky achieved that record for the most part without a manager.

Ryan's Suspension

In one of his wheelings and dealings, Tommy arranged with Al Weill for a bout between Rocky and Ernie Durando. Being in a bragging mood, Tommy challenged Weill by saying that Durando could only win by a knockout, that if the fight went the distance,

Rocky would win for sure. When Weill refuted the assertion, Tommy rebounded by asking Weill to agree that he would not stop the fight unless there was a knockout.

In his very first fight of 1952, January 11, in Madison Square Garden, with millions watching on national television, and Rocky ahead in the first six rounds, unexpectedly in the seventh, Durando unleashed a right hand to Rocky's head which send him to the canvass. Rocky stayed down until just the end of the count at which time he got up to resume fighting. Instead, the referee stopped the bout, giving the victory to Durando. Rocky's corner protested to no avail. Seeing the referee was not about to listen, Tommy jumped into the ring, ran to the referee and punched him in the mouth to everyone's surprise and amazement.

Angered by referee Miller's premature decision, and seeing there was nothing anyone could do, Rocky's entourage angrily moved to the locker room, his trainers and friends banging their fists on tables and lockers. Father Dolan, who had been ringside, followed Rocky with the hope of comforting him. On seeing the priest, Tommy, who had been swearing up and down the locker room, quickly stopped. When he saw Al Weill appear at the door, however, he lunged forward with punches and kicks, stopping only when Father Dolan stepped in between and covered Al Weill's body.

Bob Christenberry of the New York State Athletic Commission quickly suspended Ryan's license, leaving Rocky without a manager.

The fight with Joey Di Martino in Brooklyn was a Main-go contest to a packed house. Rocky also fought the future undisputed world middleweight champion— another Pennsylvania boy— Joey Giardello. The last fight in Scranton, at the famous Wattras Armory, Castellani fought the very tough fighter, Terry Moore. In March, he fought three bouts in a row: Zanelli,

Bratton and Graham.

During this time, something very unusual happened. After Sugar Ray Robinson beat Jake La Motta for the world title, Sugar Ray neglected to keep physically fit. In a bout with Randy Turpin in London, Sugar Ray lost the middleweight title— a surprise to the boxing world. However, in a return bout held at the famous Polo Grounds in New York, Sugar Ray regained his title. But, in another bout, wherein Sugar Ray was attempting to wrest the world lightweight title from Joey Maxim, after rolling up a good lead, Sugar Ray in the 14th round unexpectedly collapsed from the terrific heat. As a result, he decided to retire, leaving the middleweight title up for grabs.

The various commissions decided on an elimination tournament to obtain a successor which was going to have an effect on Rocky's career.

In spite of the odds, Rocky ended 1952 with a tremendous December 10 victory over Jimmy Flood. Unbeknown to Rocky, a very unusual fan by the name of Alvin A. Naiman was mesmerized by Rocky's convincing victory and style. He approached Tex Sullivan, telling him he was interested in getting into the boxing business, that he was interested in promoting any good young promising boxer. Tex, of course, recommended Rocky, but never believed for a moment that the stranger was actually serious.

In that year, however, Rocky did not accomplish his feats without sacrifice. Having lived with the Ryans in New Jersey, he hardly saw Mary except for some weekends, she having agreed to sacrifice until he got a shot at the title.

"But," she told Rocky one everning, "I'm not going beyond that."

She felt better when Rocky told her to continue to have patience, to live in Sworysville with her mother until he built a home in Atlantic City. Startled, she answered skeptically, "You're kidding!"

At that time, Rocky's stepbrother Birch and he

agreed to both build brand new houses side by side in Margate, New Jersey outside Atlantic City.

"I'm serious," said Rocky. "We even got the money. Are you happy?"

"Sure am! What about your manager? What's he got to say about this— not that it interests me in the least," she remarked.

"First of all, he knows about us being married. I told him about the house, and he said it was fine so long as I maintain my training schedule, which, as you can see from my string of victories, is paying off."

"I'm glad for you," she said unconvincingly. Knowing she had hurt his feelings, she threw her arms around him. "How about spending some time alone before going back to New Jersey?"

Boxing Without a Manager

Leading up to the eliminations, for eight bouts, the resourceful former marine champion took upon himself to be manager, promoter, and trainer, succeeding in ending the year undefeated.

With Ryan's suspended and Al Flora out of the picture, young Rocky Castellani decided to move into his new home and to train from there, to Mary's happiness, even if it meant sleeping in different rooms, as they did.

Doing the best he could to manage his own career, and with the help of Tony Pallone, Rocky nevertheless got some help from Tex Sullivan, who, under the table, was able to help line up some of Rocky's bouts— a practice frowned upon by individuals like the Boxing Commissioner.

Happy with the overall year's accomplishments, Rocky, Tex, Tony and several other friends and relatives celebrated the coming New Year with a party given by Rocky at his new house. For the guests, however, midnight proved a surprise. Lifting a glass of champagne, and standing next to Rocky, Mary made the toast: "To our first born, may he... or she be as healthy and as great as Rocky."

Happily surprised, they all yelled their cheers, drinking up noisily.

Chapter 15

World Middleweight Aspirations

The various commissions decided on an elimination tournament to obtain Sugar Ray's successor. In Europe, Randy Turpin, the Empire Champion, and Charley Humez, French and European title holder, were matched for a bout in London, with Turpin winning.

In America, Carl Bo Bo Olso of Hawaii, and Paddy Young of New York, leading middleweight contenders, were then billed for an American championship bout at the Garden, Olson winning.

Olson and Turpin were matched to decide who would succeed Robinson. Olson outpointed Turpin and became the undisputed middleweight champion of the world.

After winning the first bout of 1953 against Ralph Jones, Rocky was in for another unexpected setback, this time at the hands of a practically unknown French boxer, Pierre Langlois.

Be it because Langlois had a different style of boxing, or because the bout went twelve rounds— a first for Rocky, or probably because Tommy's fears were coming to haunt the married boxer whose wife was expecting, Rocky lost the bout to the Frenchman. For his entourage, it was a real disappointment; for Rocky, it seemed like a dream never to be realized. For the first time in his life, he began to feel he was not *Young Rocky* anymore. Furthermore, it was the first time the crowd booed him during the match. The only consolation was the controversy over the eleven round full count ordered Rocky by the referee, who had called his going to the canvass a knockdown rather than a slip. Furthermore, Judge Chuck Shortell gave the bout to Rocky. But, it was the overall decision that counted, and Rocky had lost.

At home with Mary, he began to express doubts about his ability to go on with boxing.

"I think I should retire while I'm ahead... At least I think I'm ahead."

"You're ahead alright. Look at you. You're in the best of health and very young."

"Ya, I feel good. I'll start looking for a job," he said, obviously disillusioned, feeling he had also let his family and friends down.

Finding a job proved to be difficult. Like so many athletes who live for their sport alone, too many of those who do not make it to the top have a hard time coping with the many demands of life. It didn't take long for Rocky— now that he wasn't fighting and drawing the money, to feel the pinch. And with Mary pregnant, the future looked mighty bleak at that.

Feeling depressed, suddenly, he felt the urge to go home, realizing that perhaps he had paid too little attention to those he loved so much. On arriving, Yolanda was quick to throw her arms around him and kiss him. The only one to have gotten a high school diploma, she was now working and seeing a young man. Mr. Castellani, who was settled down with his wife, seemed to be getting along well.

"Attilio, sono così contento... I'm so happy to see you. You're staying for supper, I hope."

"Si, resto a cena... I'll stay for supper."

"Yolanda, Connie, subito, forza. Attilio... Yolanda, Connie, hurry, come on. Attilio is staying for supper," he said as he hugged his son, while the two boys scurried around trying to grab onto Rocky's arms.

"Pop, I want to ask your opinion," he said in a serious voice, as he sat down on the sofa next to his father. "You know I lost the last fight against the Frenchman. I thought of retiring from boxing and getting a job. I've been trying, but so far, nothing. You know, Mary is..."

"Non preoccuparti... Don't worry, things will be fine. Good things always happen to you because you are a good man. As for retiring, I think it is too early. Look at you! I wish I looked as good as you, even when I was your age. Your face— it doesn't look like that of a fighter. Besides, are you going to let a Frenchman pull you down like this?"

"No Pop, it's not that."

"Do you think your mother would say quit?"

His spirit lifted, Rocky returned to Mary with a more positive outlook. Noticing the change, she commented that maybe he ought to go visit his people more often, "including my mother," she added. "She simply adores you."

A smile on his face, he took her by the hand.

Alvin A. Naiman

Naiman was a millionaire businessman from Ohio, who made his money in the wrecking business. Having seen Rocky knock out Johnny Mack in the very first round, Naiman decided to adopt the former pride of the marines. After breaking into the dressing room, he introduced himself to Rocky, who was slightly taken back by the unexpected visitor.

Upstairs in the lounge, Naiman asked Rocky what connections he had or maintained with his managers, especially with Tommy Ryan. When Rocky answered he was free and clear, Naiman then asked if he wanted a new manager. On receiving a positive response, Naiman had a hard time containing his joy. "You will never forget me. You will never regret this!"

Unbeknown to Rocky, Tommy still had a saying in Rocky's future, and Naiman knew it. However, he was able to completely buy Tommy out with an agreed sum of $20,000. Without blinking an eye, Naiman wrote out a check to Tommy with the understanding that the separation be complete.

In learning about the transaction, Rocky commented, "That's an awful lot of money, Al. I hope that I can deliver for you."

"You can by kicking the hell out of the Frenchman. You and I have a return bout," said Al.

Mary, who was always a little skeptic about good things happening just like that, became a believer when Naiman bought a nine room house in the Shaker Heights section of Cleveland and deeded it to Rocky. Furthermore, Naiman put Rocky on a regular weekly salary for working in the front office, whether Rocky went there or not. He even put Sid Terris, the trainer from New York City, on the payroll to help train Rocky.

"Rocky," Naiman said in a very serious tone, his head down a little, his eyes straight forward into those of Rocky, "the purse is all yours. I don't want any of it. You just go out there and beat that Frenchman!"

Pulling strings only as he could, Al Naiman wanted Rocky to gain the middleweight title for the state of Ohio, the only thing getting in the way being the bout with Langlois, which Rocky had to win. "You have to win this one, kid," he said during one of the training routines. "All Cleveland will be watching you."

The evening of June 17, practically all of Cleveland was present at the fight, all anxious to see the stuff Rocky was made of. Although Rocky did not knock Langlois out, he did win convincingly over the Frenchman, so much so that the crowd went crazy with excitement. Their new hero had done it in style.

Al Naiman, of course, was bursting with pride; June 17 was his birthday, and what a gift Rocky had made him. He quickly spoke with Jim Norris and set up the bout for the state title to be held in Ohio on August 22 against Jackie Keough.

In the dressing room, everyone celebrated. One reporter approached Rocky on the fight.

"Everything went your way, Rocky. Congratulations! Is there anything else you could have asked for?"

"Ya, I just wished my father had been there."

"How about this relationship with Mr. Naiman? What does all this mean to you?"

"Now that I have job security, I have no worries. My first five years as a pro, I made over a hundred thousand dollars. From all that dough, I netted only about five grands a year. Besides, I lived in several places, and I wasn't settled. My wife was afraid I'd get hurt; I had family problems. And I had to fight all the time whether I was in condition or not. I just needed the money. When I had to lay off four months with the broken hand, I had plenty of worries. And when you got things on your mind, you don't fight too good."

"So, we can look for goods things from now on?"

"I hope so. I'll sure try."

Between training and what not, Rocky did manage to spend some time at the office and in the yard, if for no reason other than to watch and learn what was going on. On one of those occasions, while walking through the yard with Mr. Naiman, Rocky noticed the foreman was having problems with the craddle hookup. Remembering his experience in Guam and Iwo Jima, where he had seen a lot of loading and unloading of heavy equipment, he suggested to use a cable-link basket instead of the craddle. The foreman used it, successfully.

"Rocky's got a life job with us. When he's finished fighting, he'll be my contact man," Naiman bragged to to the press. "He's a smart boy, just like our son Jack

Jr. I'm proud to have him in our business."

"Are you sure you won't be disappointed," she said softly.

"I don't think so. It's Rocky that I'm fond of. It doesn't much matter if he wins the championship. But wouldn't it be wonderful if he did!" he said, obviously happy. "I want to do right by this boy. I feel like a father to him. I hope you and Jack don't feel I'm overdoing it."

"Al, we like Rocky very much. He is unusual. He is talented. He is also very honest. We also like him very much."

"You know I'm planning to build a new gym, and to bring in more qualified and experienced people."

The evening of August 22, Al Naiman was ringside waiting for the bout to begin. He was slightly nervous and anxious.

"You look green, *dad,*" Rocky said, looking down from the ring. "Better I should sit down there and you up here!"

The bell soon sounded to start the fight for the middleweight state crown. Rocky started the fight deliberately slow, wanting to conserve energy for the latter rounds. During the first five rounds, Rocky concentrated on Keough's body. In the sixth, Keough rebounded with several barrages to Rocky's head, quickly establishing superiority and control, and gaining the momentum. The bout suddenly in danger, Rocky decided not to take any chances. With the seventh, he went on the offensive and quickly neutralized Keough. In the eight, Rocky scored with several powerful left hooks. In the ninth, finally, Rocky sent Keough to the canvass for a count of 9. Rocky continued his barrage until he floored Keough once again. Keough made an attempt to get up. When the referee saw him wobble, he stopped the fight. Castellani got the TKO in the ninth.

Now, the Middleweight Champion of Ohio, Rocky did not have it easy against Lombardo, a tough young man from Mount Carmel, Pennsylvania. Right in the first round, Lombardo caught Rocky on the chin and sent him to the canvass for the count of nine. Hurt as he was, Rocky fought back all the way to the end, winning the bout by a decision. He would win the next four against Ted Olla, Mickey Laurent, Gil Turner and Ernie Durando by decisions. He knocked out Phil Rizzo in the sixth, and won another ten round decision against a tough Spanish Pedro Gonzales, who gave Rocky one of the most challenging fights of his career. With that string of credible victories, Rocky felt ready to go for the world middleweight title held by Carl *Bo Bo* Olson, who had just won the crown by defeating Randy Turpin.

In the Laurent fight, Rocky literally lifted the French middleweight off the canvass when he connected with a left hook.

The combination of Al Naiman, Sid Terris and Rocky worked out well. Their successes truly responded to a team's success. With all those victories, they would go to San Francisco's Cow Palace for the middleweight championship of the world.

Preparing for the Bout

With *Ring* Magazine listing Rocky second, his name was being mentioned along with Olson, Sugar Ray Robinson, LaMotta, Graziano together with champions in the other divisions. Expectations, therefore, were high for Rocky's entourage.

Al Naiman made an offer of $125,000 to Sid Flaherty, Olson's manager, for a shot at the title; that sum constituted a record guarantee by any fighter's manager up to that time. Trainer Sid Terris and Al Del Monti, set up all of the fighters' equipment. They were also to oversee the construction of the controversial 15-foot ring for a period of six weeks. Naiman even hired Jack *Doc* Kearns— the former promoter of the great Jack Dempsey— whose skill in promoting fights was unmatched. Naiman, an amateur boxer in his youth, had no fears of gambling it all for the "Gate" and the "Middleweight Crown". "Life has all kinds of risks," he said. "I didn't get where I am by sitting idle. Things come only when one tries. After all is said and done, trying is really what counts even if winning has to be the goal. But remember, trying— always trying is what counts. Do you understand, Rocky!"

He understood. Throughout his life, he had always tried, knowing that he would continue. In tune with his patron's philosophy, Rocky trained with an assiduousness never equaled, if that were possible.

"Al," Rocky said, "I want that title more then anything in the world."

"Of course. But remember, if it doesn't come, it won't be the end of the world."

At home, he confided with Mary about the upcoming bout, telling her the importance of the match with Olson.

"Rocky, I know how much the title means to you. But look!" she said, nodding toward their baby, "nothing can be as important as the both of us."

"Yes, Mary, you know that. No matter what, you two will always come first," he assured her as he pulled up his son to hold him on his chest.

Secretly, however, Mary wished the bout with Olson would be the last. But she knew it wouldn't be so. Boxing was in Rocky's blood, and breaking away would be difficult. The only possibility— she was now convinced, was Alvin Naiman. In her eyes, he was the best thing that happened to Rocky and to her family. Through him, she saw Rocky able to have a future other than boxing. She also knew that Birch was negotiating to buy a night club in Atlantic city on the famous Boardwalk.

With Jack Naiman having made all the arrangements for the move to California, Rocky was given a suite at the Bermuda Palms Motel, where he stayed with Mary and their child, Dean. Because of the large number of people in the entourage, Mary had no problems socializing. Rocky, however, decided to spend some time away from the group. In between training, he took them to the San Francisco beaches. Lying on his back, with Mary to one side and his son Dean to the other, Rocky thought back to the Guam and Iwo Jima beaches— remembering the good times, his successes with boxing, and how proud he was to have been a marine. Now, so close to his first fifteen rounder for the title, he was thankful for all that had happened to him.

"You know Mary," he said, as though he was coming out of a thought, "even if I don't win, it won't be the end of the world. I'm confident we'll do alright. I love you so much."

With tears in her eyes, she put her arms around him, realizing the mental torment Rocky was going through. After all, the pressure was on him, and it just wasn't fair!

Rocky's entourage did every thing possible to make things smooth. They even arranged, successfully, two meetings with the champ, *Bo Bo* Olson. As usual, Rocky handled himself very well— always a gentleman, sure of himself, but never arrogant, qualities that endeared him to the press, which gave him tremendous coverage. Even the local people were friendly. A car dealer loaned him a brand new Mercury for his personal use.

The Fight

The show was staged by Jim Norris, the head of the International Boxing Club in partnership with Benny Ford.

It was the middleweigh champion's first fifteen rounder. It wasn't a sell out crowd for the title bout, but the 12,000 fans made it a good showing for the nationally televised event.

With referee Ray Flores giving his conditions on how to proceed with the fight, the two boxers went to their corners. When the bell sounded, the crowd gave a wild cheer. Rocky quickly went on the attack, knowing that as the challenger, in order to win, he would have to do so convincingly. His only worry was the length of the fight— 15 rounds. He had never gone beyond 12. As a result, he tried to conserve energy and at the same time keep the champion from getting the upper hand. With that strategy, Rocky fought well, always looking for an opening to land his punch. With the fight more or less even, in the eleventh round, Rocky finally found an opening. With a quick short right, Rocky sent the champion to the canvass. Stunned, Olson got up on the count of three. With the crowd yelling beyond all limits, urging Rocky to go for the final kill, Olson moved around in desperation, trying to avoid Rocky's blows, which, for the most part went wild. Then, instead of getting close into the champion, Rocky began defensive tactics, feeling that Olson's energy were spent, that all he needed was simply to outlast the champion. This change, however, had the fans and boxing experts suddenly perplexed. There Rocky had a tremendous chance to finish off the champion; instead, he chose to go on the defensive. Al and Sid kept on yelling to go on the offensive; but because of the noise, Rocky was not hearing the advice from ringside. Rocky needed an all out attack, which he, in view of his physical appearance, could have effected and didn't— to the incredulous crowd. Olson, always moving, missing frequently, kept stepping around the ring to confuse Rocky, hoping to avoid similar blows. Moving silently, his sight fixed on the champion, Rocky kept on throwing punches, but only occasionally connecting, especially with his right— not enough, however, to do any serious damage to Olson, who, by the sound of the bell began to feel his energy returning.

Feeling invigorated, Olson rushed to the center of

the ring for round twelve. Angry over the knockdown of the previous round, Olson charged like a maniac. Toward the middle of the round, he finally connected to Rocky's chin with a stunning over-hand right, sending Rocky to the canvass. Hurt, Rocky succeeded in getting to his feet. After wobbling toward the ropes, he collapsed again. His eyes glassy, he rested on his knees watching the referee counting "one, two, three." Then with his fingers close to Rocky's face, the referee continued, "four, five, six, seven, eight." As he was about to pronounce "nine", Rocky got to his feet. Rocky had taken the count to better able to weather the storm. That he did, and he finished round twelve. He continued for the remaining three rounds, engaging the champion, who did everything trying to put Rocky away, but failed.

Rounds eleven and twelve were the big ones, to the enjoyment of the fans who cheered wildly. Regardless of the outcome, they had gotten their money's worth and knew that this bout was one for the history books.

The title bout, of course, went the full fifteen rounds, with Oslon declared the winner.

Quietly, and with his strength all but gone, Rocky turned to the people in his corner. Wide eyed, he stared at them as if to say, "I did my best." After being consoled, and hearing the decision, Rocky proudly walked over to congratulate the world champion.

"You sure put up a great fight, Rocky. I admire you!" Olson said, still breathing heavily.

"And you're a champ," Rocky answered, stepping back away from the limelight, and from glory.

"Rocky!" yelled Naiman, "don't worry. You did great. You got nothing to be ashamed of. Your time for glory will be coming."

Rocky looked into Naiman's eyes for a long moment, trying to believe in that possibility. "I do believe I did my best, and I believe in myself and my

206

family. Let's go to the locker area. I'm tired."

While they walked through the crowd to the dressing room, the fans kept on screaming and applauding the defeated athlete. They liked his nobility and his spirit, though many believed he had made a tactical errror in going defensive after knocking down the champion in the eleventh when he should have stayed on the offensive. For that reason, many believed Rocky would certainly come back strong in the future.

That was the furthest thing from his mind. During those moments, all he wanted to do was to go to his wife and child, and to his father and sisters if that were possible. Later as he drove to his motel, he found consolation in knowing he had a place to go where he knew he was wanted and loved. On arriving, he threw his arms around Mary and his child.

"I tried Mary, I tried. That punch did me in. It hurt a great deal, more than you can imagine. I don't know how I got up, but I couldn't stay down. I'm sorry."

"Sorry!" she exclaimed. "You're *my* champion, and that's what counts."

Rocky looked deep into her eyes for a very long moment. Noticing the love on her face, he realized that though he may not have won the title, he had certainly won the crown, and they were his jewels.

He kissed her tenderly, drawing his *young* son into their embrace.

Epilogue

Except for Rocky Marciano, the Heavyweight Champion of the World who did not make a comeback after retiring undefeated, Attilio *Rocky Castellani* made an unsuccessful comeback for the Middleweight crown. In his quest for that title, he fought a courageous bout with the legendary Sugar Ray Robinson, whom Rocky knocked down for a nine count in the sixth round. Sugar Ray, nevertheless, was able to hang on and to win the bout by a split verdict.

Presently, Rocky Castellani is a successful restaurateur, a devoted family man and an active participant in matters relating to boxing.